PRAISE FOR THE FIF

'This book is a must-read for anyone in business. Allan gives you specific information to help you grow and properly manage your business, while minimising tax. It is packed with actionable advice and a dash of important mindset and human psychology principles. There is definitely something for every business owner in this book, no matter your level of success' **Pat Mesiti, Author**

'All the information I wish I'd had when I first started my business. It has solid business, money and tax advice that anyone in business should follow. Allan dives deep into key principles that will help you manage your business's cash flow and avoid overpaying taxes. Allan also openly discusses the emotional cost of running a business, which is often a hidden secret among many business owners, and how to avoid the trap of near-debilitating anxiety, which often comes with success. Read this book cover to cover – you'll be glad you did' **Steven Essa, Author**

'Essential reading for those seeking a magic formula for success that works every time or those who want to make more money and know how to keep it (by paying less tax). Allan Mason draws on experience from over 40 years as an accountant in practice and in business. As an entrepreneur, you must invest in yourself, be self-motivated to be successful in life and business, and have a growth mindset. Learning from people who have experience, knowledge and good judgement is paramount. By acting on and implementing what Allan has provided for you in this book, you will create more wealth and manage your business better, so you make more profit (and keep it). Plus, it will help you become wealthier and healthier, both emotionally and psychologically. *Tax Secrets of the Rich* is a game changer' **Lisa Fogarty, Founder, Performance Circle**

ABOUT THE AUTHOR

 **Allan Mason** is a chartered accountant, registered tax agent, registered company auditor, SMSF auditor, business advisor and the founder and managing director of Encore Accounting Pty Ltd, a prominent and well-respected chartered accounting firm on the northern fringe of Brisbane, Queensland.

He holds a practising certificate with Chartered Accountants Australia New Zealand and an SMSF specialisation. In his 40 years of public practice, he has established and operated over 15 successful businesses, including a number of accounting practices, a finance company, a financial services company, and a sawmill.

Owning a business is not always a bed of roses – it takes dedicated effort, hard work and also *smart* work. But if you make it profitable, it is certainly very exciting. As a published author of numerous books and articles, Allan has been able to pass on that knowledge to help business owners achieve their aims.

When Allan was engaged by Kerry Packer at Consolidated Press Holdings, Kerry said, 'Son, you need to be worth double what I pay you.' That message has continued to resonate.

ALSO BY THE AUTHOR

Survival to Success: How to Play the Game of Life and Win
Business Bullseye: How to Succeed in Business
How to Choose an Accountant: Your Most Valuable Team Member
Fable of a Master: Unleashing the Power that Lies within Us All

For more information on these titles,
see www.broadviewpublishing.com.au

TAX $ECRET$ OF THE RICH 2022-23

BY KERRY PACKER'S FORMER ACCOUNTANT

ALLAN MASON

HarperCollins*Publishers*

IMPORTANT NOTE
The information in this book is intended as a general resource only and may not take account of your individual circumstances. You should consult a qualified professional before making financial decisions based on this book.

HarperCollins*Publishers*
Australia • Brazil • Canada • France • Germany • Holland • India Italy • Japan • Mexico • New Zealand • Poland • Spain • Sweden Switzerland • United Kingdom • United States of America

First published in Australia in 2021 by Broadview Publishing
This edition published in 2022
by HarperCollins*Publishers* Australia Pty Limited
Level 13, 201 Elizabeth Street, Sydney NSW 2000
ABN 36 009 913 517
harpercollins.com.au

A catalogue record for this book is available from the National Library of Australia

ISBN 978 1 4607 6238 7 (paperback)
ISBN 978 1 4607 1509 3 (ebook)

Cover design by HarperCollins Design Studio
Cover image by shutterstock.com
Author photograph by Brooke Mason Photography
Typeset in Sabon LT Std by Kirby Jones
Printed and bound in Australia by McPherson's Printing Group

MIX
Paper from responsible sources
FSC
www.fsc.org   FSC® C001695

Contents

Foreword

It is not often that you come across a chartered accountant or lawyer who has 40 years' experience in business and commercial accounting, finance, and professional and taxation practice, who has also written successful books on those issues and become a qualified expert in the exciting field of superannuation. Superannuation has allowed the development of personal or family super funds that are collectively valued at over $100 million in assets from the mid-1990s due to changes by the Turnbull government in 2017.

Allan Mason is such a person. He is a pleasant and polite person, both on the phone and in person. If you ask him a question, he responds remarkably quickly with an accurate and easily understood response, indicative of a man who knows what he is talking about. With Allan, there are no 'ums' and 'ahs'.

In reading the prepublication text of his current book, *Tax Secrets of the Rich*, it seems obvious to me that Allan has developed his fluent style of writing to match and magnify his spoken words. The result is an easy-to-read text that leads to a better understanding of the complex issues that arise in relation to business transactions, protecting assets and complying with the technicalities of taxation.

The publications on business and taxation are heavily weighted on the academic side, and there are few I have encountered on the practical side that provide information for small business owners, small tax agents and small tax practitioners. This has created a significant gap on the non-academic side of single publication literature.

In my view, *Tax Secrets of the Rich* will fill much of this gap as a single publication. It provides a vast amount of knowledge, from understanding what taxation is, an examination of real cases the author has worked on successfully, the structure and use of entities set up by the owners and operators of businesses, and what makes a successful business – all in clear and concise language that will resonate with the ordinary business operator and taxpayer.

Peter Hanley LLB (University of Queensland, 1974)
Co-author, *Australian Tax Handbooks* 1989–2021

Introduction

We all hate paying tax. We see it as a necessary evil. That the taxation office is our partner in business, taking anywhere from one-third to over half of our profit or income (if employed). It is a function of modern society. With the burden of paying for the stimulus measures introduced all over the world to support businesses and the community due to the Covid-19 pandemic, this is likely to get worse.

If you believe that this is OK, then this book is not for you.

If, however, you want to be in control, keep reading. Do you want the same tips that many wealthy people have used to create their wealth, then keep it or donate it in the manner they consider appropriate? If so, you should learn from an expert in this field.

Unfortunately, the tax system has a tendency to dampen our enthusiasm to grow a business. We all see the manner in which our tax dollars are spent, and we all know there are people who receive money without working, which can lead to despair. There is a better way. Minimise your tax so you are able to help yourself, your family and those around you. Then make a conscious decision on who you will help.

I wrote this book with the desire to help business owners take back that control. It basically covers two important areas. Firstly, how to make more money, and secondly, how to keep it.

As a professional chartered accountant, I have over 40 years of experience in solving many tax issues.

This book is not a tax manual. It does not cover every aspect of taxation. It can't, as the tax act and regulations span over 100,000 pages. They are also too complicated for a non-professional. I have tried to distil the information into what the majority of people need, in simple language, in order that they may take control of their financial affairs. I have also provided case studies on how I have used the tax system to do this. I wanted to impart my knowledge and tips on what it takes to be successful in business. In my career, I have seen it all. From massive success to massive failure, and even situations that have led to suicide.

In life, you can learn from other peoples' mistakes or learn from your own. Eastern religion tells us that it might take 10 lifetimes to learn from your own mistakes to reach perfection. My aim is to reduce that for you.

Part 1 deals with why money is important to get right. It begins with understanding and playing the tax game, being proactive with different structures, and includes comments from Australia's richest man (in the 1980s) about tax and wealth. It outlines basic facts about money, the power of compounding and how to increase your wealth (so you have a tax problem for accountants to solve).

Part 2 outlines the tax system in Australia, the money raised each year and the manner in which the Australian Taxation Office goes about ensuring there is integrity in the system. In other words, how they ensure they catch any unreported income. It dispels the myth that taxation is an exact science. It is not. There are many loopholes, incentives and ways to use the system to your advantage. But you must do so legally and with caution. Post Covid-19, be aware that 2022 will be a tax catch-up year, where taxpayers will be asked to pay back the tax stimulus measures the government introduced during the pandemic. There are some eye-watering figures (deficits) shown here.

Part 3 is all about finding a strategy that will save you tax. It's all about knowing tax law, knowing the incentives available, and knowing how to adapt your situation or transaction to the tax laws in a tax advantageous way. The key word here is to adapt, especially if there are two ways to do something and one of those results in less tax being paid. This section lists 11 areas of taxation with tax tips that are unique to each different application of tax law in different business or personal situations. As mentioned earlier, tax can be complicated, but I am trying to make it simpler to understand.

Part 4 explains the secrets to success at a business or personal level. It explains the formula for running a successful business and things every business owner should know and apply. If you follow these rules, it will guarantee success every time. It includes eight vital money tips for running your own business. Tip 8 is an especially important chapter that lists what most Australians have done to never be dependent on any form of financial assistance.

Part 5 deals with the physical, psychological and emotional aspects of running a business. On a positive note, it covers having a millionaire mindset. As a business owner you are the leader of your business. This chapter highlights the mindset you need to have to lead your business. On a negative note, it covers how to handle the adversity and knockbacks that every successful person experiences. In many cases, this means being at the top of your game one day and being knocked to the floor the next. This section looks at how to handle this rollercoaster ride and importantly discusses the very real impacts and consequences of extreme stress on entrepreneurs – on their personal relationships, their health and mental health. It also highlights some of the warning signs of being 'financially trapped'.

From early adulthood, in addition to attending university to obtain a Bachelor of Business (major in accounting), I read self-help books profusely, ranging from Steven Covey to Dale Carnegie, Anthony Robins, Brain Tracey and many more. I have listened to tape series from the best and attended numerous seminars, all of which have helped me gain more knowledge and insight into what it takes to be successful. After all, what better place to invest in than yourself?

In 2009, I wrote *How to Win the Game of Life*, a self-help book based on what I know from experience works.

The purpose of *Tax Secrets of the Rich* is to show you how to make more money and keep it. While we all focus on tax-saving ideas, in this book, I outline ways to actually change your mindset, so you have a more positive and abundant view on life and success.

Is there a magic formula that you can apply that will work every time to make you lots of money, so you can lead a fulfilling and rewarding life? Part of that formula is dealing with the intangible and emotional factors that affect us all. As emotional human beings, life affects us in different ways.

Life throws challenges in our path. Self-sabotage, marriage break-ups, recessions, financial crises and pandemics all play a part. Taking a saying from the film series *Mission Impossible*, 'Your mission, should you choose to accept it,' is to overcome these challenges and push through them to achieve the greatness that is within you. Every successful person has needed to overcome adversity in some form to take them to a level they never thought possible. If it was easy, everyone would be able to do it. Hopefully, this message (or tape) will not self-destruct in two minutes.

This is your test. Are you up to the challenge? And yes, there is a magic formula to success that works every time, and this book will help you find it.

Part 1

Understanding Taxes and Money

Money is an important medium of exchange. It is necessary to buy the necessities of life. To live a fulfilling life, you need to have enough money to meet your needs and the needs of your family. In retirement, you need a nest egg that will continue to achieve the same aims. Many people who are not financially successful will argue otherwise. They'll claim that you can lead a meaningful life on a government pension. After all, you have paid tax all your life, so now is the time to get some of that back. Sadly, this is simply not true.

The focus of this book is maximising your personal wealth and retaining it for the above reasons. I should also add that this means obtaining wealth legally and ethically. I know many situations where wealth has not been attained legally or ethically, which only results in its loss. It is a fact that when wealth is not obtained this way, you cannot seem to hang onto it. Also, it is no fun having free board and lodgings at Her Majesty's pleasure.

This section deals with some basic facts about tax and money, the power of compounding and leverage, and how to hold onto it. It also covers what some wise people have said about taxation and why you need to look after your own retirement and not be reliant on others or the government to do so. Given the current situation the Australian economy is in (and, in fact, the entire world), Australia will be funding the current deficits for many years to come. The Covid-19 stimulus measures have cost the government billions in borrowed money. Pensions have never provided nor kept pace with a reasonable standard of living. Things are about to get worse.

Being self-supported and financially wealthy will allow you to help those less fortunate than yourself. You cannot do this if you do not have the means to do so. Being wealthy enables you to be an important contributor to society, both in terms of your own spending and by being able to help others who, for various reasons, need assistance.

How you allocate your wealth must be your decision, not one forced on you by others, like the government.

1

Taxes Set to Rise in 2022 – The Start of Repayment of the Tax Stimuluses

Time to pay the piper.
Robert Browning

Just a word of warning about the tax system both in Australia and worldwide. Every reader will have suffered through the worst pandemic in history, a period of unsurpassed change and adjustment, and a period when all financial caution was thrown to the wind and rightly so, as life and death situations need to prevail in times of crisis.

But we are now past that. It will be time to pay the piper, as the saying goes. 'Paying the piper' means that governments will need to work towards balancing their budgets. Balancing the massive deficits that were the result of the above. Reducing long-term debt and balancing inflows with outflows. You can imagine what would happen if, say, your income was $100,000 per annum and your expenses $140,000 per annum. You cannot sustain that for long. Countries do go bankrupt and countries do need bail outs. It has happened all over the world with catastrophic effects – take Greece, for example.

What will that mean to the average taxpayer? It means you must, more than ever, be diligent about your own personal wealth and wealth creation. A major part of this will be minimising your donation to consolidated revenue. To paraphrase what Kerry Packer said, the government doesn't (or didn't during Covid-19) spend your money too wisely, therefore you should not be donating any extra.

Call me sceptical, but I believe immediately after the election, the treasurer (whoever that might be at the time) will insist on the government addressing these shortfalls. In Chapter 9, I cover what these shortfalls are. They are massive; eye watering, in fact. An overrun in expenditure exceeding to 30 per cent of the total tax collected.

Simplistically, a government solves its tax shortfalls/deficits in three ways:

1. It prints money to increase the money supply, which has the effect of inflating itself out of its mess. In non-economic terms this means making current dollars worth less. Think of it like a cake. You divide the cake into 10 pieces and each piece is 10 per cent of the cake. If you print more money, you effectively could divide it into, say, 100 pieces, which means each piece is now only 1 per cent of the cake. Your money is eroded, buys less. Inflation will occur, as now there is more money in the system. The problem is some sections of the economy will benefit from inflation, while some will not. Those on fixed incomes usually lose, while those in business that can increase their prices will keep pace. There are lags that cause losses and catch-ups. Also, with inflation, taxation will increase in absolute (not real) terms. In an extreme example, say the average wage goes from $100,000 per annum to $1 million per annum but doesn't buy any more because prices have increased. The $150 billion deficit is now watered down to $15 billion in future dollars that are worth less.

2. It raises income tax. Creating a special levy is not new. Former Prime Minister Julia Gillard decided to raise the Medicare levy to help fund the rollout of the National Disability Insurance Scheme. This wouldn't be the first time governments have turned to levies to meet a deficit. Under John Howard, they were used to fund the famous gun buy-back scheme and help pay for defence costs in East Timor. Then, after winning the election in 2014, the Abbott Government felt the country was in such bad shape that it introduced a budget repair levy of 2 per cent. It would not surprise me to see this happen again in late 2022 or 2023. Look out for a Covid-19 repair levy to increase taxation to help repay the massive handouts given out during the pandemic. Expect it to be anywhere from 3–5 per cent and last for a minimum of two years.

3. It reduces spending. In other words, it reduces the amount of money it pays out on social welfare, schools, education, etc. Politically, this is very difficult. A government, if it wishes to be re-elected, has great difficulty reducing what it previously pledged to provide. Instead, what it does is to not increase the above in line with inflation and cost-of-living increases. This has the effect of reducing the real costs of amounts paid. You can expect that this will happen.

Of course, there are lots of other small measures a government can do. Things like improving compliance with more taxpayer audits, and amending or removing offsets and various rollover relief measures. For instance, it could decide to tax superannuation at a higher amount, remove the 50 per cent capital gains tax (CGT) concessions, remove rollover relief when you sell a business, etcetera, etcetera. This list is unending.

The Australian Tax Office (ATO) each year reviews what it calls the tax gap. This is currently estimated to be around $33.5 billion or 7.3 per cent of tax collected. It is defined as being the difference between what the ATO considers the tax collections should be and what they actually are. In other words, it is an estimate on how much tax is not being paid for various reasons, like the cash economy, overseas companies using transfer pricing and other non-compliance tactics business or taxpayers may utilise to illegally evade tax. The government usually gives the ATO extra money to increase audit activity in areas it feels may yield a return. Lowering this tax gap is one such area that may help reduce the deficit.

What usually happens is the government engages a task force to review all tax measures and come up with a number of recommendations.

All of this means that you, the taxpayer, need to be diligent in tax planning as, more than at any time in history, this will be vital to manage. Taxes are on the increase and guess who will be the victim of these increases? It will be the average taxpayer, the average worker, the small business owner. They always seem to be hit hardest. I therefore encourage you to take a proactive position and do not allow yourself to be a victim.

2

The Tax Game

For most people, taxation is about simple mathematics, and it is not subject to dispute. Many accountants are so busy that they see their job as simply tallying the income, then deducting the expenses to arrive at a net income. They then look up the tax payable in accordance with the tax tables. It's a mechanical exercise not subject to any discretion.

Too many taxpayers also see this as the situation. The more income they earn, the more tax they pay, and that is how they think. I even hear clients say they want to limit their income and hence limit their tax. My answer to this always is that you never pay 100 cents on the dollar in tax.

But getting back to the income-tallying exercise, the government want you to believe that there is no discretion. They want you to believe there is nothing you can do. Tax is an inevitable part of life. As the saying goes, there are only two things that are certain in life: death and taxes. While this might be partly true, the fact is that there are many thousands of accountants who more than pay their way by coming up with smart solutions to prove the above is not correct. Yes, there are many who are simply form filers, but in all large firms, the testimonials are that a smart accountant has saved a client substantial sums, making the client forever indebted to them. I know that I have, on many occasions, pulled a metaphorical rabbit out of the hat. I have even surprised myself sometimes. In this book, you will see how the wealthy (many of whom were my clients) have reduced their tax, including some actual case studies.

My point is that taxation is not an exact science. It is not a mathematical equation from which the tax payable drops out the bottom. It is very subjective and capable of being worked to the taxpayer's advantage. This is what all wealthy (and some not so wealthy) people do.

When you read this book, you will understand some of the tricks that I have used to help my clients reduce their tax payable. After over 40 years as an accountant to many household names and many wealthy people, I will highlight what I have been able to achieve for my clients. It becomes a game. A tax game that an experienced person can often win at.

After all, if taxation is an exact science, why does the ATO sometimes lose in court? Why do they need over 100,000 pages of legislation, rulings and guidelines on the taxation effect of the many issues that businesses face?

The trick is to be creative. Know the rules and use them to your advantage whenever possible. Be a step ahead of the game.

3

What Kerry Packer Said about Tax

While working for Kerry Packer, we were always conscious of minimising any taxes payable. When Kerry engaged me back in the 1980s, he said, 'Son, you need to be worth double what I pay you.' That message has always stayed with me. With Consolidated Press Holdings (CPH), and with my current clients, I was often able to minimise their tax payable. What Kerry said still echoes in my ears.

I can clearly remember one situation at Consolidated Press when Kerry received a tax assessment of something like $178,231.78. At the time, we were using a number of structures, and the tax office disagreed with our structure and our tax returns lodged. They issued an amended assessment as above. When we received the assessment, Kerry's instructions – after a few choice swear words and 'who do they think they are?' comments – were to send them a cheque for $1.78. 'That's all they F'n deserve.' The matter went to court, and we won the case. I remember that during the time in court, Kerry was very calm, collected and professional. I think he knew we would win. Kerry always employed the best professionals, whether that was accountants, lawyers or barristers. The tax office was completely outgunned.

One of the barristers acting for the tax office, being a bit smug, asked our barrister, 'What do you want us to do about the $1.78?'

Kerry overheard this and replied in a loud voice for everyone to hear, 'You keep the money; you need it more than I do!' You can imagine everyone in the courtroom laughed, as Kerry, in his quiet manner, had again shown he was the boss.

He proved later that his sayings would live long after he did. One of his most famous sayings came when he was before a Senate committee who were enquiring into his tax affairs. Today, there is a moral and social obligation to pay your fair share of tax, which goes beyond the letter of the law. But in those days, it was fair game to minimise your tax in whatever way possible. It was for the high court to decide if such a strategy would be successful. In many, many cases, the high court ruled in favour of the taxpayer. It was a different world then. This was before the days of Fringe Benefits Tax, Bottom of the Harbour Legislation and Part IVA Schemes, which were introduced with the sole intent to reduce tax.

So, it was of no surprise when Kerry was requested to appear before a Senate committee on taxation to be asked why he minimised his tax the way he did. Kerry's appearance and reply is, to this day, still viewed on the internet. I even have it on my website, as I worked for Kerry at this time. I clearly remember the allegations being laid against him. The press even stated he had criminal connections and tried to discredit him. They said his underworld name was Goanna, being a form of lizard. This was totally wrong and unfounded. It would later be proved that someone had simply invented it. But the pressure caused him to stand up for himself. Kerry had never been good at being the public face of the company and he hated the media. This was despite the fact that, at that time, he owned numerous newspapers, magazines and a television station (Channel 9). On this occasion, however, he decided to respond to the pressure. I know that at CPH, a lot of time was spent preparing him for the likely questions that could be asked. When he took the stand, part of his reply, which would go down in history, was, 'The government doesn't spend my money too wisely; therefore, I am not contributing a cent more than I absolutely have to, and anyone that doesn't structure their affairs to minimise their tax should have their head read.' Meaning, of course, they were insane or should visit a psychiatrist.

The senators were dumbfounded. They did not know what to say. They didn't know how to reply to this. In the meantime, Kerry very casually stirred his cup of tea. The room was so quiet you could hear a pin drop. He had won the day. The press had a field day, and to this day, this quote has appeared in numerous articles. I am sure you, as the reader, have heard it.

So how do you pull a rabbit out of the hat? How do you build wealth for the future without being hamstrung by losing half of it in tax along the way? Planning is the key. Sometimes transactions can be structured different ways. Sometimes you need to step back and consider the impact of what you are contemplating, review the laws and look for a better outcome. This book will give you many ideas and many tricks that you can use to do just that.

4

The Importance of Tax Planning

MYTH:

**The more money I make,
the more tax I pay.**

Based on the previous chapters, various testimonials and case studies contained within this book, the above is simply not true. Of course, those who expect businesses to pay their fair share, the tax office and other people who are suppressed by the system all believe this. But I can say that, as an accountant in both public practice and working in industry, it is simply not true.

Let me first explain some simple examples of why the above is not true. Hint: consider the tax planning aspects of these (which will be covered later in this book):

- In Australia, (in most cases) you do not pay tax on gains associated with your sole and principal residence.
- You do not pay capital gains tax (CGT) on any increase in the value of motor vehicles.
- You only pay tax when a gain is realised. In other words, when you sell the asset.
- Capital gains on the sale of an investment property or other investment assets may be eligible for a 50 per cent

CGT discount, if you hold them for more than 12 months (hint, hint).

- Capital gains on the sale of a business may be eligible for a 50 per cent active asset discount.
- Capital gains on the sale of a business may be rolled over into superannuation to make the gain tax-free (subject to certain rules). This can even eliminate the balance of any gain after the active asset discount.
- A superannuation fund pays no tax on income earned or capital gains when in pension mode. If in accumulation mode, the tax is limited to 15 per cent on income and 10 per cent on capital gains (subject to various rules).

The above are examples of some of the concessions available. It is a summary and does not cover all situations, as there are many more concessions available, where profits are not taxed. Every situation is different, and concessions can be lost if you are not careful. For instance, if your sole and principal residence is rented out or you move overseas, the above concession can be reduced or lost entirely.

There are many, many more concessions. The main point is that just because you earn income, it is not true that you will be taxed on it.

That is why I stress throughout this book that you need to be on the front foot with tax planning. Clever structuring and planning can reduce and, in some cases, eliminate any tax payable. Planning can also use some of the above to reduce or eliminate any taxes payable. As stated, these are only a few of the concessions available. There are many more.

To repeat what Kerry said, 'The government doesn't spend my money too wisely, therefore I am not paying a cent more tax than absolutely necessary'. It is not how much money you make that is important; it is how much you keep. With tax as high as 47 per cent or more, it can become hard to get ahead. It can be hard to manage your affairs so that you keep below the tax thresholds or to save for your future retirement.

Having had Kerry Packer and many other high-net-worth people as clients, I know what these people think about tax, and how they use the system to their advantage. They never accept the status quo, they never accept that nothing can be done; they're always looking, challenging their advisors to find a way around the system to make it work for them.

For example, in 2004 we were involved in the purchase of a sawmill for around $8 million. The vendor had purchased the mill post CGT (1985) but had a low-cost base. He was facing a massive tax bill if he sold. He was considering pulling out of the deal. Instead, we came up with using the merger/demerger provisions of the tax act. The effect was a total tax-free sale.

In another example in 2018, we had a mining client who owed the tax office in excess of $1.2 million. We were able to totally walk away from that debt.

So how do you, as a small business owner, take advantage of the system? How do you use the system to your advantage?

We all know that not one system fits all that to be effective. You need to know how to use the tax system. Let me give you some simple examples on how you can tailor a transaction in accordance with the system.

Firstly, some simple rules. In most cases you pay tax on realised gains, not unrealised. So you have a chance to defer the taxing point.

Secondly, expenses incurred in earning that assessable income are generally deductible.

Thirdly, there are many tax exemptions that can apply, from prepayment rules, CGT discounts, roll over benefits, sole and principal residence, etc.

My point is that you need to stand back from a transaction, in the same way we did with the sawmill. Think about better ways to handle it and think about the concessions that may be available to reduce any taxes payable. Amend the structure of the transaction if you can. Be proactive and get advice early. Don't hand to your accountants a fait accompli. Involve him/her in the early stages. Quite simply, that is how the wealthy reduce their tax. They plan, get advice and amend as needed.

5

Business and Tax Structures

When you start a business, you have the choice of which structure to use. Many people are confused with this, and even accountants can get it wrong. Unfortunately, it is also the case that what may be the right structure when a business is started may not be the right structure as it matures.

Each type of structure has different tax and legal consequences. The type of structures available to a business owner are listed below. This is a very simplistic outline. The tax consequences are covered in more detail later in the book. The aim at this point is to give the reader an overview, without getting into the finer legal or tax consequences and complexities:

- **Sole Trader** – simply put, a person registers an ABN (Australian Business Number). They are the owner. A business name will be registered with ASIC showing that person as the registered proprietor. All liabilities vest with the business name owner. All assets owned by the registered proprietor, who is usually a person, are at risk and can be attacked. Tax is levied at their marginal tax rates.
- **Partnership** – same as the above but consists of two or more persons or entities. All partners are jointly and

severally liable for all debts of the partnership. This will not be in proportion to their partnership interest, but each and every partner will be equally liable for all debts. Profits are distributed to the partners in accordance with the partnership agreement. If no agreement exists, then profits will be distributed equally. This income will be added to any other income they have earned and will be taxed at each partner's marginal rate of tax. If partners are added or leave, the old partnership ceases and a new partnership is created. This will have capital gains tax implications.

- **Company** – meaning a proprietary limited (Pty Ltd) company. This is a company registered with the Australian Securities and Investment Commission (ASIC) as having a share capital, directors and a constitution confirming the rules that apply to its operations. The company is liable (not the directors or shareholders) for all debts, except where certain laws can pierce this corporate veil and attack the directors personally. Tax is levied at from 27.5 per cent, reducing to 26 per cent in 2021 and 25 per cent in the 2022 tax year, or 30 per cent, depending on whether the company is a base rate entity or earns passive income. New shareholders can come and go without affecting the business but may trigger the loss of any carried forward tax losses.
- **Discretionary Trust** – must have a trustee and beneficiaries. All profits must be distributed to beneficiaries (usually natural persons) to avoid high tax. Liabilities sit with the trustee, who will indemnify themselves against the trust assets. Tax is at the beneficiary level, which is usually family members. Losses are trapped in a trust and cannot be passed on to beneficiaries.

- **Unit or Property Trust** – similar to the above, but instead of having a discretionary option in respect of profits, the unit trust must declare profits in accordance with the units issued by the trust to the unit holders (similar to shareholders). Losses also are trapped in a unit trust and cannot be passed on to unit holders. A property trust will have slightly different rules regarding profit distributions and is used to retain the land tax thresholds in the entity.
- **Superannuation Fund** – usually referring to a self-managed superannuation fund. A superannuation fund can, in certain instances, operate a business, although this is very restricted. Super funds can be in pension mode or accumulation mode or both, depending on the members of the fund. Tax, when in accumulation mode, is 15 per cent, and 0 per cent when in pension mode. Legal liability rests with the trustee. A super fund is governed by the rules of the Superannuation Industry Supervision Act. Hence, it is very regulated, must be audited and compliance costs are higher.
- **Other structures** include public companies, public trading trusts, not-for-profit entities and various other charitable trusts. These are outside the scope of this book.

6

Tax Rates Using Different Structures

In the midst of chaos, there is also opportunity.
Sun Tzu, *The Art of War*

Trading as a company, sole trader or through various other types of entities will result in very different rates of tax being paid. In my experience, business owners do not pay as much attention to this as they should. It is also important to understand that sometimes you can use multiple entities to minimise your tax.

For example, you could pay yourself a wage from your company up to the tax-free threshold and the company tax rate. Then leave the balance in your company, which will be taxed at company tax rates. Hence, if you are a base rate entity, the maximum tax payable both for yourself and your company can be as low as 26 per cent in 2021, reducing to 25 per cent in 2022. But the first $18,200 paid to you (and your spouse), for work done, as a wage will be tax free.

If you have an asset protection trust, you can pay a licence fee to this entity, which can then be distributed to beneficiaries that may have a low income and take advantage of the tax-free thresholds or low-income tax rates applicable to them. Alternatively, you can also maximise your superannuation contributions (up the limits available) for all family members who work in your business and pay this into your self-managed superannuation fund. Just simple examples of how to play the tax rate game to your advantage.

Playing the tax rate game is what all good accountants do. They look at the situation, step back and come up with solutions. To play this game means having a thorough understanding of the taxes payable by different entities and through different structures. As mentioned earlier, sometimes situations change and what may work at one period in your business cycle may not work later. Be flexible. Consider your options but more importantly be proactive in making decisions. Listed below are the tax rates that apply to various entities. Use and know this like the holy grail.

Figure 1 Tax Rates for an Australian Resident 2021–22

Taxable income	Tax on this income
$0–$18,200	Nil
$18,201–$45,000	19 c for each $1 over $18,200
$45,001–$120,000	$5,092 plus 32.5c for each $1 over $45,000
$120,001–$180,000	$29,467 plus 37c for each $1 over $120,000
$180,001 and over	$51,667 plus 45c for each $1 over $180,000

Source: Extracts from the Australian Taxation Office (ATO) taxation tables.

The above rates do not include the Medicare levy of 2 per cent, and/ or the Medicare levy surcharge. The surcharge applies if you do not have hospital cover.

Figure 2 Tax Rates for a Non-Australian Resident 2021–22

Taxable income	Tax on this income
0–$120,000	32.5 c for each $1
$120,001–$180,000	$39,000 plus 37c for each $1 over $120,000
$180,001 and over	$61,200 plus 45c for each $1 over $180,000

Source: Extracts from the Australian Taxation Office (ATO) taxation tables.

Company Tax Rates

In a very simplistic way the government introduced a two tax-rate system for companies on the 23 August 2018. This affected the rate of tax companies pay from the 2018 income year to the present. The terms 'base rate' and 'passive income' were introduced. Loosely speaking, providing a company's passive income is not more than 80 per cent of its assessable income, the lower tax rate will apply. Passive income includes rents, royalties, net capital gains, interest, dividends, trust and partnership distributions. But, as always, the devil is in the detail and the above is not quite as simple as it sounds. I have seen many situations where the finer detail of the definitions of passive income give a different outcome than expected. The definition of assessable income can also be important and how you divide the assessable income based on the above.

As mentioned, from the 2017–2018 income year, companies that are base rate entities are taxed at the 27.5 per cent company tax rate, reducing to 25 per cent as per the table below. If your company does not qualify as a base rate entity, it will be taxed at 30 per cent. The lower company tax rate applies to base rate entities with an aggregated turnover of less than $50 million from the 2018–2019 income year.

With a bit of careful planning you can ensure you meet the less than 80 per cent rule. Don't get caught out and pay a higher tax rate if you can conform to the above base rate entity rules. It is always better to pay tax at, say, 25 per cent (for the 2022 tax year) than 30 per cent. If you are unsure, check before the year ends and maybe defer certain passive income such as interest or rent payments (if possible).

Below is a table from the ATO website defining the above:

Figure 3 Progressive Changes to the Company Tax Rate

Income year	Aggregated turnover threshold	Tax rate for base rate entities under the threshold	Tax rate for all other companies
2017–2018	$25 m	27.5%	30.0%
2018–2019 to 2019–2020	$50 m	27.5%	30.0%
2020–2021	$50 m	26.0%	30.0%
2021–2022 and future years	$50 m	25.0%	30.0%

A base rate entity is a company that both:

- has an aggregated turnover that is less than the aggregated turnover threshold, which is $25 million for the 2017–2018 income year, rising to $50 million for later years; and
- 80 per cent or less of their assessable income is base rate entity passive income.

Base Rate – Passive Income is Defined As:
- dividends, which also includes the franking credits attached to them
- rent and royalties received
- interest income
- gains on certain shares or securities
- any net capital gain
- income received from a partnership or trust that can be traced to having a base rate entity passive character.

Tax Payable by Superannuation Funds

A complying superannuation fund pays tax at 15 per cent on both earnings and concessional (tax deductible to the payer) contributions received. This will apply while the fund is in accumulation mode. When the fund moves to pension mode, the fund is totally tax free. This means all capital gains and profits earned are totally tax free. Yes – you read this right, totally tax free.

Superannuation has massive benefits on how you fund your future retirement. The system was introduced and continues to be used as a vehicle to shelter income and reduce tax. Many young people have trouble seeing the future benefit as they tend to focus on a short timeframe. There is a lot of regulation surrounding superannuation because of these tax benefits. But do not be afraid to consider this. This is covered in more detail later in this book.

Tax Payable by Trusts

Again this can be a confusing area. But in reality, it is not. Think of trusts as a flow-through entity. Unless you want the trust to be taxed at the top marginal tax rate (45% + 2% Medicare levy), a trust must flow (or distribute) all its profits to its beneficiaries. Hence, tax is levied to the beneficiaries at their marginal tax rates. Trusts have benefits, but they do not suit every situation and there are traps to be careful of. The main disadvantage is that losses are trapped in a trust and cannot be distributed. The main advantage is that you can play the tax rate game more easily by paying profits to low tax rate beneficiaries. This is covered in more detail in the tax tips section of this book.

7

Case Study Using Different Structures

A Sole Trader

When a business operates as a sole trader, the registered proprietor, which is usually a person, pays tax at their marginal tax rates.

Take the following case study:

Mr Plumber came to me to discuss his tax, complaining that he seemed to be paying too much. His friends were saying how little they were paying, and he felt he was being ripped off (using the words of the plumber). He had a net income (after expenses) of $180,000.

The tax he was paying was as follows:

Tax on $180,000 (2022 tax year) was $51,667, plus a 2 per cent Medicare levy of $3600, making his total $55,267. This assumes he has private health insurance. If he doesn't, he will also pay a Medicare levy surcharge of an additional $1800. The total is an eye-watering $57,067, or an average tax bill of 31.7 per cent.

In addition to the above, the plumber, as a sole trader, will be required to pay quarterly instalments based on the last year lodged (indexed by inflation, which was suspended for the 2020–2021 year). This is called Pay As You Go Instalments (PAYGI). Hence, he will be paying quarterly instalments of $57,067 / 4 = $14,267.

No wonder the plumber seemed concerned. If the above was his first year of trading, and if we assume the financial year we are reviewing was the year ending 30 June 2022, his tax payable in 2023, based on his 2022 tax, would be $57,067, plus four instalments for the 2022 year as a catch-up of $57,067, bringing us to a total of $114,134. Based on an income of $180,000, this represents a massive 63.4 per cent. Of course, Mr Plumber didn't have $114,135 to pay to the taxation department. He had spent all his net income. This first year can be crippling and needs to be carefully watched. I have seen it lead to massive tax problems that could have been avoided if addressed quickly.

A Company

Let's assume the above case study for Mr Plumber. He makes $180,000 profit. Instead of leaving him as a sole trader, we incorporate him into a company. Some accountants and bookkeepers do not suggest this as the costs to run a company are higher. After you read the following, you will change this view. Trading through a company will also have some legal liability protection, which means his personal assets will not be at risk, should some unforeseeable event occur.

In a company, we will assume he does the following:

- Takes a weekly wage of the equivalent of $80,000 p.a. His tax is deducted from his income and is forwarded each month to the taxation office.
- He pays superannuation on his salary, plus a bit extra to a total of $15,000, which is well below the $25,000 threshold. Being young, he does not want to go too far with super.
- Pays company tax on the balance of $85,000 and leaves it in the company for future growth, to buy a new car, tools, plant and equipment, etc.

His tax will be as follows:

- Personal tax, which is deducted from his salary and paid monthly to the ATO: $18,067 p.a.
- The super fund will pay 15 per cent tax on his super contributions: $2,250. He won't even see that as the fund will automatically pay it. The money will be held by the super fund in his name, earn income and accumulate to provide for his future retirement.
- The company will pay tax at 25 per cent on $85,000 net profit (being a trading or base rate entity): $21,250.
- The total tax payable in this situation will be $18,067 + $2,250 + $21,250, for a total of $41,567. A saving of $15,500.

The above also eliminates the personal PAYG quarterly instalments (of $57,067 noted earlier) that Mr Plumber had to pay, being the double tax in the first year. This helps with Mr Plumber's cash flow planning. The tax saved far outweighs the costs of incorporating. There are also some other advantages which can be client specific. In the first example, Mr Plumber has a massive tax and cash flow problem looming. He had a false sense of income and wealth and was on the path to a massive debt ($114,134) problem. It's a problem I have seen many times – one that could have been avoided with planning and forethought.

A Trust

I was asked to review the taxes of two valuers who were trading through a unit trust. The units in the unit trust were owned by their two discretionary (family) trusts. The unit trust did not pay them wages but instead they took trust distributions. At the end of the year, the net profit of the unit (trading) trust was paid to the unit holders, being the two discretionary family trusts. This net profit was the accounting net profit, so from a cash point of view, it did not always get paid out. This was because the unit trust sometimes had cash flow issues due to the receipt of money from clients.

The two discretionary family trusts distributed the profit they received to their beneficiaries. The owners of the business received their remuneration as distributions from the family trust. Also, spouses and other family members received distributions.

You can see the income splitting that was happening and possible tax reductions due to this structure, which is very common. It is something we often use, but it does have cash flow problems.

The owners were complaining that they seemed to be paying too much tax and were always behind with their tax liabilities. Take the example mentioned above with the plumber and the PAYGI system. This can cause problems when incomes rise and can be a constant cash flow nightmare. They complained that they never seemed to be able to get up to date.

While it is a common structure, it has two major problems. Firstly, with trust distributions, the ATO requires a payment in advance based on the prior year lodged. Quarterly PAYG instalments must be paid. Secondly, the owners are employees and should be paying themselves a base wage with tax deducted at the source and superannuation being paid. This greatly improves cash flow.

However, the main point of mentioning this case study is to do with asking questions. It's essential to know your client and get to know as much as you can about their business. When I started to ask questions, they told me about valuation software that they had been working on. Over the last five years, they had spent money on this software and hoped to market it at a great profit. They were even using this software in their business. The software was created in a separate entity and had accumulated large tax losses. My eyes lit up.

On the one hand, they were struggling to pay their personal taxes, but on the other hand, they had invested substantial sums into this software development. From a tax perspective, they could use these losses in their current business. This was something that had not been looked at by their current accountant. How? Quite simply, they could charge a licence fee. They were already using and testing the software, so why not pay for it? They already had a licence agreement they were hoping to use for other clients. We simply put this in place for the trading company, charged an upfront fee and, in one year, we recouped over $100,000 in taxes. In one transaction all of their tax debts were wiped.

A Super Fund – Running a Business

You may not know that a self-managed superannuation fund can run a business provided it is for the sole purpose of providing retirement benefits to its members. But when is it appropriate for your needs, and how do you ensure the fund remains a complying super fund? Why would you do this?

A super fund in accumulation mode pays 15 per cent tax. When in pension mode, it pays no tax (providing certain conditions are met). So, there is a massive advantage.

Consider the following scenario: an elderly person at pension age needs a little extra to live on. She has some assets and is relatively fit, but she doesn't have enough income to live on. The return on her superannuation balance is so low that to fund a reasonable lifestyle, she will need to draw against capital to do so. This will quickly deplete her superannuation balance and be a problem later in life, especially if her health declines. She decides that through her super fund, she will acquire the goodwill of a bed and breakfast/short-term accommodation rooming house. There are no loans, and the operation is run cash flow positive. Let's assume the business earns $150,000 per year. Being in a tax-free environment and meeting all the rules, this income is totally tax free. As the fund is in pension mode, she is of pension age and the fund is a complying self-managed superannuation fund, she can draw a weekly pension from her super fund to live on. As she has complied with all of the rules as listed below, the pension payment is totally tax free. The net effect is that no tax is paid on any of the income of the fund, nor the pension payments withdrawn.

The following requirements need to be reviewed and adhered to:

- Ensure the sole purpose test for the fund is not breached so as to retain the eligibility for tax concessions.
- Ensure the business accords with the super fund's investment strategy (which, of course, can be written so that is does comply).
- Must meet other regulatory requirements:
  - Commercial arm's-length investments
  - Loans and financial assistance
  - Assets from related parties and arm's-length dealings
  - Borrowing
  - Ensure the members of the fund's individual circumstances are considered
  - Weighing up the pros and cons of using this structure.

Clever structuring and a set of circumstances that fit the criteria make this structure an ideal vehicle to earn income tax free.

8

How to Grow Your Wealth – The Power of Compounding

It is said that compounding can make you rich. Very few people truly understand what compounding means and how to use it. The reason it is important to consider, at this early stage of this book, is that by taking control of your money, you have a chance to make it grow. When you fail to adequately plan for taxation or any other major expense and lose half of it, the ability to compound your wealth and grow it is severely limited. No matter what you think about taxation and paying your fair share, this simple fact can make it very hard to create the financial freedom you may wish to attain. It helps ensure you are not in need of any form of welfare to help you survive in the future.

In Australia, it is a sad fact that 95 per cent of the population will retire broke. By broke, I mean without sufficient income to live on and without some form of financial assistance or support. This support usually comes from either family or government. Some consider it a rite of passage when they get older to be able to still qualify for an aged pension. Well, wake up, Australia! The cost of pensions to the government, as our population ages, will be such a drain on the economy that the government will be forced to reduce the pension. If it is not reduced, it will simply not be increased in line with CPI, which will have the same effect over time: reducing it to below the poverty line. When the aged pension was introduced in 1900, less than 5 per cent of the population lived beyond 65 years old. Today, the reverse is true. How the government will fund a future pension that enables a person sufficient income to survive is very unclear. Given the pressure on the public purse due to the Covid-19 support packages, it is highly likely that the government will be unable to sustain anywhere near the current levels of social welfare. The solution is to look after yourself and to not rely on a government handout that will simply not be there.

So, what is compounding and how does it work? As a simple example, think about the median house in Sydney. In 1970, it was $18,700. Today, the figure, post-Covid-19 is edging close to $1.5 million. In just over 50 years, it has increased by an eye-watering 7,921 per cent. I use this example as it is true compounding.

Compounding, by definition, is earning interest on interest. Adding the interest to the principal and earning further interest on that new principal. If you compound monthly, the result is greater than if you compound yearly.

Let me explain a simple example to illustrate my point. You apply for a job. The employer offers you either $1 million if you work for them for 30 days or to give you a cent a day and double it every day for 30 days. What would you choose? Which pay option will give you the highest income? If you take the $1 million, that is all you will get. But let's consider the cent-a-day option. 1 cent becomes 2, becomes 4, becomes 8 becomes 16. After eight days, it is $2.55. After 15 days, you will have received only $327.67. You are starting to think that with half the month gone, the $1 million upfront would have been the best option. It is slow initially, but it really builds up. It gives you exponential growth. This is what happens with compounding. After 30 days, your total income is $10,737,418.23, or at 31 days, it is $21,474,836.47.

Look at the table below. This is the true power of compounding. It is almost unbelievable, but as an accountant, I can tell you that figures do not lie.

Figure 4 The True Power of Compounding

Day	Amount	Total
1	$ 0.01	$ 0.01
2	$ 0.02	$ 0.03
3	$ 0.04	$ 0.07
4	$ 0.08	$ 0.15
5	$ 0.16	$ 0.31
6	$ 0.32	$ 0.63
7	$ 0.64	$ 1.27
8	$ 1.28	$ 2.55
9	$ 2.56	$ 5.11
10	$ 5.12	$ 10.23
11	$ 10.24	$ 20.47
12	$ 20.48	$ 40.95
13	$ 40.96	$ 81.91
14	$ 81.92	$ 163.83
15	$ 163.84	$ 327.67
16	$ 327.68	$ 655.35
17	$ 655.36	$ 1310.71
18	$ 1310.72	$ 2621.43
19	$ 2621.44	$ 5242.87
20	$ 5242.88	$ 10,485.75
21	$ 10,485.76	$ 20,971.51
22	$ 20,971.52	$ 41,943.03
23	$ 41,943.04	$ 83,886.07
24	$ 83,886.08	$ 167,772.15
25	$ 167,772.16	$ 335,544.31
26	$ 335,544.32	$ 671,088.63
27	$ 671,088.64	$ 1,342,177.27
28	$ 1,342,177.28	$ 2,684,354.55
29	$ 2,684,354.56	$ 5,368,709.11
30	$ 5,368,709.12	$ 10,737,418.23
31	$ 10,737,418.24	$ 21,474,836.47

Let's now look at this with an interest factor of, say, 5 per cent and bring to account the effect taxation will have on your rate of return.

From your school days, you will probably remember the following formula for compound interest:

$$A = P(1 + \frac{r}{n})^{nt}$$

Where:

A = equals the amount you will end up with
P = the original principal amount
R = rate of interest as a decimal
N = number of periods (12 for 12 months or 52 for 52 weeks)
T = time in periods (months or years)

For example, you have $1000 earning 5 per cent, compounding monthly for 15 years.

This becomes A = $1000(1+(0.05/12))*(12*15)
A = 1000 ((1.00417)*(180))
A = $2113.70

Hence, it has doubled in 15 years, earning a mere 5 per cent rate of return. Imagine if, along the way, there were a few years where the interest was, say, 10 per cent. This could reduce the doubling time to only 10 years. Imagine if, at the end of each year, you lose 30 per cent of the income in taxation. This will extend the doubling period to in excess of 20 years.

This is why, at a personal level, superannuation, property and other long-term assets, if retained long enough, can give you the above eye-watering gains. As mentioned earlier, consider the example of the Sydney property. An investment of $18,700 in 1970 is worth $1,500,000 today.

Now you understand the power of compounding, you need to use it to accumulate wealth.

George S Clason, in his book *The Richest Man in Babylon*, covered this very point. It was first published in 1926 and continues to be a best seller. It is about how small savings accumulate wealth over time. It is as true today as it was in 1926. I recommend that everyone read this book.

Part 2

Why Tax is Not an Exact Science

The case studies that follow are actual situations that have occurred in my career in working with my clients. They highlight the various tax issues our clients have faced in their business. Real situations that show how even the well-intentioned can get it wrong. Given that the ATO may challenge a position taken, it indicates that there is often a difference of opinion on who is correct. Since the tax office sometimes loses, this also indicates that the tax office is sometimes wrong. My $1.78 example with Kerry Packer is a good illustration of this.

I have seen the ATO take a hard line when they are clearly wrong. I have seen assessments issued that are wrong in law and fact. I had one case where a plastic surgeon client received (in about 1990) a large refund to which he was not entitled. Because we managed his tax so well, we needed to reduce his gross wages to the PAYG deducted. Hence, his net pay was zero. When I discussed it with the tax office, they couldn't see the error, even though I tried to explain it to them. The client ended up keeping the refund with the knowledge that he may have to give it back. He never did.

My point is that there are 125 different taxes in Australia with over 100,000 pages of legislation, rulings and case law (enough paper to reach from the floor to the ceiling). The Income Tax Act of 1997 consists of 12 volumes. No one can be expected to get it right every time.

In the past, tax was treated as a game. With the right professional advice, you could do many things to minimise your tax.

Sir Garfield Barwick, as chief justice to the High Court in Australia (the highest court in the land), confirmed this in a speech on 12 April 2005: 'The liability to pay income tax is wholly derived from the law imposing and providing for the assessment of that tax. The obligation to pay it is a legal one. Some politicians try to treat it as a moral obligation. But it is not. The citizen is bound to pay no more tax than the statute requires him to pay according to the relevant state of his affairs.

'Consistently with this view, it has long been a principle of the law of income taxation that the citizen may so arrange his affairs as to render him less liable to pay tax than would be the case if his affairs were cast in some different form. In the language of the layman, the citizen is entitled to minimise his liability to pay tax. This is sometimes expressed as a right to avoid tax, an expression which is in contradiction to the evasion of tax, a failure to pay tax which is properly due.'

Of course, Kerry Packer expressed the same view in 1991 when he was called before the Australian Senate.

There has been some erosion of the above with the introduction of the general anti-avoidance provisions incorporated with Part IVA of the *Income Tax Assessment Act*. However, the point is that a person has a right to use the law to minimise their taxation; to use various structures, processes and systems to pay the minimum tax possible; and to obtain professional advice to achieve that aim. Something I have been asked to do many times.

9

The Taxation System in Australia – Balancing the Budget

Ever wondered how much money the government raises from taxation and how it is spent? After all, it is your money being allocated to various programs decided by others (the government).

In the ATO Annual Report for 2021, there were 11.8 million individuals who paid tax and 4.3 million small businesses, including sole traders. In respect of the wealthy, there are 201,000 privately owned wealthy groups that cover 952,500 entities (which means the wealthy have on average 4.7 entities each). Of course, the above are the published figures. But I know many individuals who never make any of the above statistics. Hence, the true figures are far greater.

Total revenue collected for 2021 was $582 billion (2020 was $537 billion), less refunds given of $129 billion (2020 $132 billion), resulting in a net tax collection of $453 billion (2020 $404 billion). To collect this revenue, the ATO employed 21,281 (2020 was 21,184) people as of 30 June 2021. Their actual expense for 2021 was $4 billion, of which 50 per cent related to wages ($2 billion). Hence, based on the above collections, they raised $453 billion, which cost them $4 billion to raise, resulting in a profit or amount available to consolidated revenue of $449 billion (2020 was $401 billion).

For the last three reported years (2019, 2020, 2021), total collections by the ATO were as follows:

Figure 5 ATO Net Tax Cash Collections, 2018–19 to 2020–21

Tax	2018–2019 $m	2019–2020 $m	2020–2021 $m
Gross PAYG withholding	204,764	214,426	220,457
Gross other individuals	48,423	43,713	48,769
Individual refunds	−29,514	−36,219	−36,265
Total individuals	**223,673**	**221,920**	**232,961**
Companies	93,590	83,971	98,636
Superannuation funds	11,269	6267	12,956
Resource rent taxes	1053	1052	786
Fringe benefits tax	3794	3850	3569
Total income tax	**333,379**	**317,060**	**348,908**
Excise	23,300	23,352	24,462
Goods and services tax (GST)	65,270	60,296	73,094
Other indirect taxes	1657	1529	2033
Total indirect taxes	**90,227**	**85,178**	**99,589**
Major bank levy	1560	1612	1619
Superannuation guarantee charge	577	674	1040
Foreign investment fees	94	94	88
Self-managed superannuation fund levy	144	127	134
Total net tax collections	**425,980**	**404,745**	**451,379**
Other revenue	−59	−386	1418
Total collections	**425,921**	**404,358**	**452,797**
HELP/SFSS	2915	3416	3754

Source: 'Table 3.1, ATO net tax cash collections, 2018–19 to 2020–21', Commissioner of Taxation Annual Report 2020–21, p 58.

Based on the 2021 Government Budget for 2022, the government expects revenue from taxation to climb to $482 billion (see page 76 of the Budget Papers). This is expected to rise by $107.1 billion per year to 2024. The upward revision in revenue is quoted as being due to:

'A stronger economic recovery and elevated iron ore prices have supported company tax receipts and domestic consumer spending has supported a strong rebound in GST receipts. The rapid recovery in the labour market has supported higher personal income tax receipts. Over the latter half of the forward estimates period, an improvement in the outlook for employment is expected to drive higher prices and wages growth, further supporting personal income tax receipts.' (2021 Government Budget, page 125).

Of course what is not said is that the ATO will step up its collections by trying to close what they call the 'tax gap', a gap in what it perceives as being the true tax payable on income earned. In other words, stricter compliance measures.

If we analyse these figures, as a taxpayer, the ATO does a great job of collecting money. It costs around 9 cents in the dollar to collect taxes. A very low cost of sales – one that would be envied by any business owner. The government is then charged with spending that money. This expenditure is outlined in the following table:

Figure 6 Estimates of Expenses by Function

	2020–21 $m	2021–22 $m	2022–23 $m	2023–24 $m	2024–25 $m
General public services	33,037	26,070	24,811	25,148	25,830
Defence	33,375	34,473	36,496	38,344	40,721
Public order and safety	6712	6652	6074	5889	5919
Education	42,604	42,799	43,496	44,626	46,010
Health	94,533	98,283	95,779	99,300	103,177
Social security and welfare	225,394	209,975	214,655	219,028	224,512
Housing and community amenities	6953	7869	6283	5517	5028
Recreation and culture	4405	4532	4151	3959	3938
Fuel and energy	9090	9638	9546	10,069	10,567
Agriculture, forestry and fishing	4014	4483	3779	3280	2450
Mining, manufacturing and construction	4394	4354	4230	4138	3739
Transport and communication	13,828	14,460	17,618	16,411	13,322
Other economic affairs	83,819	14,640	11,091	10,103	10,068
Other purposes	97,279	111,106	117,368	128,853	138,414
Total expenses	**659,437**	**589,334**	**595,378**	**614,665**	**633,694**

Source: 'Table 6.3: Estimates of expenses by function', 2021–22 Budget Paper No. 1, Budget Strategy and Outlook 2021–22, p 161.

Figure 7 Expenses by Function in 2021–22

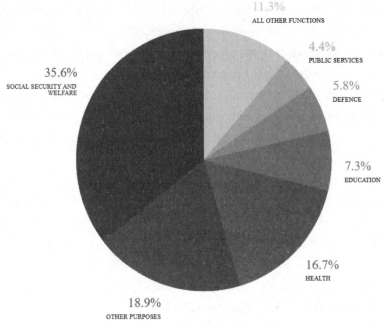

Source: 'Information from chart 6.2: Expenses by function in 2021–2022', 2021–2022 Budget Paper No. 1 Budget Strategy and Outlook 2021–2022, p 163.

If we bring together the ATO collections and the government spending, we can clearly see that net collections are $452 billion, with actual expenditure in 2021 of $659 billion (shortfall of $207 billion). For 2022, the ATO expects to collections to be $482 billion. With planned expenditure as above projected at $589 billion, a deficit of $107 billion is projected. These deficits will continue to add up and as noted below will result in a net debt of $1.2 trillion by 2025.

The population for Australia is currently running at around 26 million people, of which only 14.2 million are registered taxpayers (according to the page iii of the 2021 ATO Annual Report). While there are some timing differences on when these numbers were ascertained, only about 55 per cent of the population are registered taxpayers. The balance is more than likely children, non-working partners, social welfare recipients or people who do not lodge a tax return for whatever reason.

At a macro level, it is also important to know the future of taxes raised in Australia. For the year 2022, it is projected that there will be a net debt of $729 billion (being some 34 per cent of the Australia's estimated gross domestic product (GDP)). This is estimated to rise to $1,199 billion, or $1.2 trillion, by 2025. The government will be challenged on how to afford to repay or even cover this debt, given tax revenue as above averages $480 billion with expenditure, as per Figure 7 above. Hence the one-third of the population working and paying tax will be forced to shoulder this burden for many years to come.

It is worth knowing where your taxation dollar goes and what the government is likely to do in 2022 and beyond to reduce the above deficits and borrowing. Post-Covid-19, governments will be tasked with doing this. A country cannot continue to overspend its collections and must eventually balance its budget.

Australia's debt level remains low compared to most developed countries. It is not surprising that debts have increased as the government, through the pandemic, needed to support the economy. However, the time is rapidly approaching for the government to begin the steps to balance its budget and repay debt. Generally a government will do this by doing three things:

- Raising taxes. This may mean additional new taxes, increases in current taxes or reductions in concessions. As mentioned earlier, it may also mean a 'Covid Repair Levy' of say 4 per cent – my words. Over the next two to three years, expect the tax revenue to increase at least 30 per cent from the current levels of $480 billion to around $625 billion.

- Reduce spending in real terms, meaning inflation-adjusted terms. Governments lose elections if they attempt to actually reduce their spending, but if they hold their spending at prior year levels and allow inflation to reduce it in real terms, this will be less noticeable.
- Printing money to increase money supply. This will increase inflation and reduce the value of money. It will also stimulate the economy in certain sectors and have a negative impact on any fixed price arrangements as they struggle to pay with current dollars. Those on fixed incomes or government support will struggle as their dollar will buy less. This is more palatable than reducing pensions or social welfare, which would be folly for any government. Instead, it will simply erode the value of money to achieve the same effect.

In most cases, a government will do all of the above, depending on what the voting public will accept at the time. But how will it trade out of $1 trillion dollars when at best it can hope for a surplus for $10–$20 billion in a great year? To even make a dent on the debt, the surplus needs to be more than $100 billion. Remember, that is on tax revenue at present running at, say, $500 billion and expenditure of a similar amount. It is just inconceivable how Australia will ever achieve a surplus sufficient to repay the above debt legacy.

In the 2022–23 Federal Budget, the government announced an additional $652.6 million to be provided to the ATO Tax Avoidance Taskforce. This increase will be for 2 years to 30 June 2025 and is expected to raise an extra $2.1 billion. This is the start of measures indicated in dot point 1 above. It will get worse.

For those taxpayers who are employees, planning for your own retirement will become more and more difficult. For employees, tax is taken first (under the PAYG system) and they are left with the balance to work with. Being proactive and on top of your numbers will, over the next 10 years, become more and more important. Otherwise, you may end up being in the 95 per cent who require financial assistance in your old age. Financial assistance that will simply not be sufficient to live on.

My entire point is to take control of your wealth. Use the systems outlined in this book to build wealth and use the incentives and tax offsets contained within the tax system to its fullest to minimise any tax payable thereon. This applies both at a business level and a personal level. If you are an employee, save as much as possible to begin investing in assets that will grow in value. It doesn't happen overnight, so be patient.

In summary, act in a proactive way to be ahead of the system and ahead of the majority of people who are simply on a mouse wheel to nowhere. This point is purposely mentioned many times throughout the book to try to help you, the reader, realise that you need to get ahead of the pack. The above figures paint a dire picture of the ability of government to continue to provide any form of meaningful support; a warning to not rely on government support that will keep you in poverty.

10

Timing of Income and Expenditure

Good fortune is what happens when opportunity meets planning.
Thomas Edison

The case studies below show that tax is not an exact science. Good fortune also happens when you take affirmative action. You do not accept the status quo. You question and look for answers. Hence, you make your own luck.

Case Study – The $732,000 Magic Trick

In about March 1990, I had a client who struck gold (figuratively). He had been working on an anti-ageing cream for a number of years and the double-blind studies came up extremely positive. Being a great marketer and having links to the advertising industry, he was able to get a spot on a television show that highlighted the major breakthrough and how it reversed the signs of ageing. His creams were able to penetrate the skin and improve its elasticity and thus reduce wrinkles.

In March of that year, his profits had soared through the roof. With over $3 million in the bank, he approached me about the tax payable. Quite simply, he told me that this would not last. He needed to put the above profits back into research and development to come up with new products. My initial view was that it would be impossible. He had made the money, received it and it was in the bank. It would have been impossible and unwise to spend it on frivolous ventures, and any R&D would need to be carefully considered over the next two to three years. But I thought, *there must be a solution.* He was facing over $1 million in tax. Remember, this was in 1990, when $1 million was probably closer to $3 million today.

Kerry Packer's words were still ringing in my ears (be worth double what I pay you, son). Having left Consolidated Press Holdings to go into practice on my own, I needed to think laterally. I needed to pull a rabbit out of the hat. I had done it before, but I needed to do it again.

The first thing I did, as a professional, was consult a few larger city chartered firms. I thought they would surely know more than I and have some ideas. After over a month of research into different things, I came up with a total blank. Most simply said, 'You have made the money; the tax is payable.'

I discussed this with the client, and we bounced back a few ideas. At this time, the ATO had introduced a section in the tax Act to allow prepayments to be made. There were restrictions that involved the business turnover and a 12-month rule. I thought maybe I could use this idea to achieve what we needed to do.

After a lot of work, a separate arm's-length company was used to act as the supplier of future services. Basically, the structure was to pay this entity for services that would be delivered over the next year, but to pay them in advance. My client physically paid all these amounts before 30 June. The future billing for media advertising would be billed and paid by this arm's-length company. They would receive a service fee for arranging and managing these services.

Without going into the finer details, which were quite elaborate and required contracts to be entered into, the structure worked. Instead of paying over $1 million in tax, the tax bill was around

$268,000. The services were rendered in future periods and the amounts paid in the normal course of business.

My point is that when the impossible seems to face you, with creativity, sometimes you can pull a rabbit out of the hat to perform feats of true magic. The above is a real-life example of a situation I solved by thinking outside the box.

The point of the above is: when is income treated as income for tax purposes and when is expenditure treated as expenditure for tax purposes? The average person would think the above needs no explanation. But that is not the case.

Our tax system, both at a balance sheet level and at a profit and loss level, allows different treatments. For a small business, you are allowed to treat income on a received basis (cash) or on an invoiced but not paid basis (accrual). This allows a business owner to (subject to various rules) treat invoices prepared on, say, 30 June but paid in July or August as belonging to either the current or the following financial year. Of course, this will only be a timing issue, as next year they need to be brought to account. Both the paying entity and receiving entity (especially if at arm's-length) can treat each differently. But if you are clever, if you know your figures and know what the current financial year is looking like, you may have the ability to defer income or conversely take up the expenditure. By knowing your figures before 30 June, or as you approach the year end, you can make decisions that can defer and effectively save a lot of tax. This is what I did for my client in the example above. By deferring any profit to a later financial year, you have a chance to either manage it better, pay additional expenses like personal superannuation (up to the limits) or at least not have to find the money until you have received it from your clients. In the case above, my client invested in massive research for new products.

11

ATO Data Matching – Their Ability Review

It can be very important when you adopt a tax position on something to know how long the ATO can go back and review that position. In other words, how long they have to amend or challenge the tax payable as a consequence thereof. This is sometimes called the 'hold your breath' period.

Case Study 1

One of our clients asked that we prepare the personal income tax returns for his mother and father. In this case, his parents had sold a rental property and needed to calculate (and pay tax on) the capital gain. They said they sold the property in September 2018. We had great difficulty obtaining information as their record-keeping was poor. After some time, we eventually obtained all the details and drafted their tax returns. This was in February 2020. Everything was completed and we were about to lodge their 2019 income tax returns. Then, we received a letter from the ATO seeking to amend their 2018 income tax returns. The letter stated that they had sold a property and had not declared the gain. The ATO had already calculated the capital gain. They knew the cost, the sale price and had even estimated items like stamp duty, legal costs and the agent's commission. When we checked, it was the same property that the client thought they had sold in 2019. When we approached the client, they finally obtained from their lawyer the settlement statement. The contract of sale was dated June 2018, the property settled in September 2018. The client did not remember the contract date and did not realise that the capital gains tax event is based on the later of either the date of the contract or the date that the contract becomes unconditional, if there are conditions that must be met, like a finance clause.

The point is that the ATO knew about the sale. They knew all of the items that made up the capital gain and were able to assess a gain with a reasonable amount of certainty. In the above case, there were a few things missing, but they were around 80 per cent right with their numbers.

What is Being Matched by the ATO

The ATO has data matching systems that provide information that can be cross-checked against any taxation returns you lodge. They are currently in their 17th year of data matching. Every year, they get better and better at it. The current specific areas of data matching activities include:

- all banks and financial institutions
- all government agencies, which include Centrelink, Child support register, Department of home affairs and immigration
- share brokers
- real estate agents for rent received and sales of property
- land titles offices in all states
- credit and debit cards of banks and other providers
- specialised payment systems
- online selling (eBay, etc.)

- ride-sourcing
- motor vehicle registries for the sale and purchase of all vehicles with a purchase price of over $10,000 (they match this against your income tax return to see if your lifestyle is at odds with the vehicles you buy)
- cryptocurrency and various online wallets being used
- overseas government agencies
- the Department of Foreign Affairs to check your residency and movements in and out of Australia.

If you have a financial transaction, rest assured that the ATO will know about it. My advice is not to hide it. Be proactive and declare it. See a professional and get help on how to minimise the tax payable. But don't simply hide your head in the sand and hope the ATO won't catch up with you. They will. The above even applies to a sale of your sole and principal residence, which is tax-free. The ATO will know about the sale, so you need to declare it and nominate that it is tax free because of the above exemption. The ATO computers do not always pick up that a sale is tax-free and may issue you a nasty letter. Worse, if you have changed your address a few times and the ATO can't find you, they may, in error, issue a default assessment and start legal proceedings against you. Before you know it, you may have a tax debt and a court-imposed penalty that can be costly in legal fees to fix.

We had this happen to a client who was prosecuted for failing to lodge several years of outstanding tax returns. Such prosecutions are a criminal offence and show up on your record. The client was unaware of this until he applied for a loan. He approached me and, after some research, I discovered that one of the years claimed as outstanding had been lodged. I advised the ATO, and they set about reversing the conviction. As it had gone that far, this process required a pardon signed by the Governor-General. When the client received the pardon, he framed it. To this day, it sits on his wall.

My point is: be aware that the ATO can sometimes go down a path without you realising it.

We are presently seeing the same with cryptocurrency. It takes time to catch up, but 'please explain' letters are starting to come out in respect of 2020 crypto transactions, some two years after the event.

ATO Right of Review

After you lodge your income tax return, the law limits how far back the ATO can go to amend your tax return. For most taxpayers with simple affairs, the tax office can go back two years, while if your tax affairs are more complex, they can go back four years.

You are also far more open to the historical scrutiny of the ATO if you fail to lodge or knowingly lodge a false tax return. In such cases, there is no limit as to how far the ATO can go back. It is therefore important to actually lodge your income tax returns on time or even early, as the time limit may preclude the ATO from making an amendment. We work with a legal firm in Brisbane that refers to this as the 'hold your breath' period. Remember, even with full disclosure, sometimes the law is not certain on what can be claimed. This is illustrated by the fact that the ATO often has cases they lose. So, interpretation can be key. But if the ATO lose their right to amend due to the above time restraints, there can be no amendment.

Case Study 2

We had the above exact situation occur with a new client. The client was a beneficiary of a trust and, as such, needed to declare the income distributed to him by that trust. The trust tax return was lodged through a different accountant. Subsequently, the ATO reviewed the trust and disagreed with the treatment of certain items. However, because all the beneficiaries, except my (new) client, had lodged their income tax returns prior to the expiration of the review period, they could not amend them. However, my (new) client's tax return was lodged within the four-year period of review. The ATO reviewed it and amended his tax return. The result was an extra $260,000 in tax. He fought it but was unsuccessful. He felt he should make a claim against his previous accountant for being slack finalising and then lodging his tax return. He stated all the information had been provided to the accountant who sat on it for over 18 months. Had it been completed and lodged promptly, the ATO would have been outside their review period and unable to amend it. A $260,000 lesson on timeliness (or tardiness).

Every year that the client brings his work to me, he mentions the above issue and complains about the cost to him of the previous accountant's tardiness.

It is therefore in your interest to keep your lodgements up to date and lodge on time. It is your responsibility to lodge your income tax return on time. If you have delegated this to someone else and they have not complied with it, it is up to you to ensure compliance. It will be you, the taxpayer, who can be fined for late lodgement. It is also good practice to lodge your returns in a timely manner as you never know when an issue may arise, particularly if you are in business, that might come back to haunt you.

12

Why You Must Do Things Legally – The Penalties

As this is the last chapter in the section, I want to make it clear that you must keep on the right side of tax law. I also want to cover what happens when you don't, are subjected to a tax audit and the penalties that can follow for not doing so.

Most would be aware that Al Capone, the famous gangster, was convicted on 17 October 1931 on five counts of income tax evasion. He was held liable to $215,000 in fines and interest on his back taxes and sentenced to 11 years in jail. It was the only offence they could convict him of, even though he is reported to have commissioned numerous deaths and was involved in racketeering in the days of prohibition in the US. The point is that when all other avenues to catch him failed, tax evasion could still be proved and resulted in his downfall.

In Australia, as in most other Western countries, the various taxation departments are said to have more power than God. They have the ability to search records from any external source and even assess you on a deemed level of income to push the onus of proof back to the taxpayer to disprove it. Hence, if the ATO issued you an assessment based on, say, $1 million in income, it is up to you to prove they are wrong and argue what your true income is.

I had a client who was subject to an audit back in the 1990s. He ran a number of ski lodges in Thredbo and Jindabyne. He had numerous rental properties, a large house and substantial assets. We prepared his tax returns based on the information given to us.

The ATO decided to audit him and requested we provide a cash flow and asset betterment schedule over the previous five years. An asset betterment is where you list the assets and liabilities each year in a table and compare them to the year before. At the bottom, you calculate either the increase or decrease in net assets. You also look at cash flow to show how any increase in assets has been funded. Needless to say, the increase in assets acquired each year did not match the available cash flow generated or declared by his business as profits.

Usually, at a meeting with the ATO, the first thing the auditor says is something like, 'Have you anything to declare that has not been previously declared? Do you want to make any disclosures?' Any such voluntary disclosures at this point may reduce any future penalties. The client had disclosed to us during the preparation of the asset betterment reports some false name bank accounts, which had not been previously disclosed. We disclosed these. The ATO officer then said, 'Do you have anything else you wish to disclose?' The client said there was nothing else. The auditor then said, 'What about this account in the name of XX?' The client went pale.

The audit went on for over a year. The fines and penalties were in excess of $1 million. The ATO then recommended the matter to the Director of Public Prosecutions. The client was jailed for eight years.

We believe someone at the bank had told the ATO about all the cash transactions and false name bank accounts. The point is: the client was either too arrogant or too crazy to realise when his time was up. Had he come clean when the audit started, he may have simply been fined and ordered to pay the back taxes. But he chose to push his luck.

We had a similar situation with a client who had a restaurant in Surfer's Paradise. At the audit, the tax officer made the same statement about disclosures. He came clean and disclosed a bank account (that the ATO said in the audit that they did know about), and he was simply fined.

So, firstly, if you are being audited, don't think that the ATO will not know what you are doing. Secondly, help them do their work. In the Surfer's Paradise example, we prepared amended business activity statements (BAS) and tax returns to correct the statements previously lodged. When the disclosures were made at the audit meeting, we passed these across to the auditor. We made their job easy. In the end, we were even successful in getting interest and the majority of fines remitted.

If the tax office commences an audit, more than likely, they will have completed their homework in advance. This happened with a restaurant client in Manly.. The ATO sat out the front of the restaurant and counted the number of patrons entering the restaurant. By the time they advised of the audit, they had already obtained all the bank account transactions from all bank accounts associated with the business. They had looked at the owners' assets to ascertain if there was a mismatch between their reported income and the assets they owned. The ATO would have reviewed any unexplained increases in net worth that were out of line with the reported net income. They would also check the social media accounts for any lavish lifestyle indicators, such as trips, holidays, cars, etc. The taxation office has the power, the resources and the time to do their job in as detailed a manner as they see fit.

As mentioned in a previous chapter, the ATO's right of review is two years if full disclosure has been made or four years for business transactions. If you fail to disclose income, there is no time limit. But the onus of proof becomes harder.

In addition to the tax (and any interest applicable), the tax laws authorise the ATO to impose administrative penalties for conduct such as:

- making a false or misleading statement or taking a position that is not reasonably arguable
- failing to lodge a return or statement (BAS, FBT, etc) on time
- failing to withhold amounts as required under the PAYG withholding system (like PAYG on wages or contractor payments)
- failing to meet other tax obligations (like superannuation).

Penalty provisions are there to encourage all taxpayers to take reasonable care in complying with their tax obligations. The ATO will often consider any extenuating circumstances when deciding what action they will take. Remember, if you help the ATO, rather than hinder them, they will be more lenient. The ATO auditors are people and have emotions. Insulting them, attacking their professional integrity and insulting the tax system are all counterproductive actions. They have a job to do – one that, to them, is very serious and professional. They are the protectors of the government revenue.

Penalties are based on penalty units, which were to be indexed each year. From 1 July 2020, the value of one penalty unit was $222. This is still the current amount. Various offences carry differing numbers of penalty units that can be automatically charged. You then have the option to apply for remission, either in full or in part, if, say, there were extenuating circumstances surrounding your situation.

For example, the number of penalty units a taxpayer could be liable for will be calculated based on three criteria:

- Not taking reasonable care – this will cost you 20 penalty units or currently $4440. This will be where you have made a false or misleading statement that a reasonable person would have not made. In other words, you have not checked to ensure what you are claiming is reasonable.

- Being totally reckless – this will cost you 40 penalty units or $8800 at the current rates. To incur this the ATO will need to show you have made a statement or a claim that a reasonable person would have checked to ensure its accuracy, that a reasonable person would have made inquiries and ensured what is claimed is not misleading. In other words, you have shown a total indifference to the facts and the law.
- Intent to defraud – this is an intentional disregard of the law. You know the claim is incorrect and yet still make it. This will cost you 60 penalty units or $13,200. If you are a significant global entity (SGE) they will double this fine.

The above is really confusing and we have had many arguments on these definitions. This is where you need to treat the auditors with respect, otherwise they can take an unreasonably strong view on this. The above base penalties can be reduced or increased if there are mitigating circumstances. This will happen when you tell lies to the auditor or fail to disclose something that takes them more time to uncover. As stated above, they are people with a job to do. If you make it easier, they will make your life easier.

Also remember that with all penalties and fines (like traffic fines), they are not tax-deductible.

The times we have been successful in ensuring no penalties were imposed were because we were able to argue that the position taken was reasonably arguable. In other words, the area is a little grey and we highlighted that.

In addition to the above, the ATO, trying to be really fair, introduced some safe harbour provisions. If you provided correct information to your tax agent and they made an incorrect statement to the ATO, you will not be penalised.

Penalties can also be based on the tax avoided. Penalties can be 100 per cent of the tax avoided, with interest being charged on both the penalties and additional tax levied. The 100 per cent additional tax can be reduced based on the three parameters listed below. Such additional amounts can be reduced to 75 per cent, 50 per cent or 25 per cent. We have seen a tax debt created after an audit increase by over 200 per cent due to the above, especially if the tax goes back a number of years. A base penalty is calculated as a percentage of the shortfall amount and can be reduced by the behaviour that led to the shortfall amount.

- Not taking reasonable care will cost you an extra 25 per cent of the tax avoided.
- Being totally reckless will cost you an extra 50 per cent of the tax avoided.
- An intentional disregard of the law will cost you an extra 75–100 per cent of the tax avoided.

So, like the restaurant in Surfer's Paradise, if you have that knock at the door, be smart. Get help. Don't think that hiding will work. Don't think that insulting the tax auditor or telling them stories will have any effect. We had a building client who confided to me that after the audit was complete, and after many years of trading, they were far more in front than they were behind. Remember, the tax auditor is simply doing their job. They see your tax dollars as public money that needs to be protected. In other words, it is not your money.

In a recent case, an accountant/tax agent told a tax auditor that they should commit *harakiri*. Needless to say, that accountant is no longer in practice. The client, who received eight years' free board and lodgings at Her Majesty's pleasure, should have learned a lesson. When you are playing a hand of poker, you need to know when it is time to throw in your hand if the odds are against you.

So, be intelligent and make smart decisions, but always treat an audit with respect.

The ATO are not always right, and we have many times successfully challenged a stance taken. We have in many cases been able to argue for much higher remissions than the above statutory penalties indicate. In the case of the Surfer's Paradise restaurant we were successful in obtaining 100 per cent remission of all interest and penalties. This is especially the case when hardship applies. But most importantly, get professional help. After all, we have seen it all before, heard all the stories and so has the tax auditor.

Part 3

Tax Tips to Save You Money

Fortune favours the bold.

Virgil

This section outlines some specific tax tips that are available to you to reduce the tax you pay. With all such tips, you need to check that these will apply to you personally. Everyone's personal situation will vary. Even a slight variation can result in a different outcome. Be aware that laws change. Governments have a habit of changing the rules, so be careful. Ensure you check the current rules and that any strategy works in your personal situation.

Throughout this book, I have continually discussed tax planning. For example, if, in a particular year, you have made a capital gain on, say, shares that will give rise to a large one-off tax bill and you also have some unrealised losses on other shares, it may pay to sell the loss-making shares to even out your capital gain. You can always buy them back after 30 June. There are some rules to be mindful of that are covered in the share portfolio section, if you use this strategy.

My point is, think and plan ahead. Taxation can be a costly mistake if you get it wrong. After all, isn't that what this book is all about, being proactive with your tax position? As I have said many times, it is not how much money you make that is important, it is how much money you have left after taxation.

13

Tax Tip 1: Your Sole and Principal Residence

I mention this first as, for most Australians, this will be your biggest tax haven. I know you may not think of it that way, but the truth is there is no tax payable on any gains you make on your family home. For this reason, many people put a lot of effort into creating an asset that increases in value. The net effect will be a retirement nest egg that may pay for your retirement when you downsize to something smaller or even move to a retirement home.

There is no reason why you cannot use this tax-free status to grow your asset base. Do not be content with buying a house and sitting on it for 30 years. Continually upgrade your position, renovate, improve, sell, buy again and do the same.

The following are some case studies on how this has worked for myself and people I know, examples of how they have set out to use this tax-free status to build wealth. I also mention some traps to be careful of.

In 1979, my wife and I purchased a house in Earlwood in Sydney's Inner West. We paid $36,000 for that house. It needed a new kitchen and bathroom, as well as some external landfill to level the block. We spent around $15,000 on renovations. We sold that house in about 1985 for $85,000, a profit of $34,000. We purchased our next house in Belrose on the Northern Beaches, paying $106,000. We spent around $50,000 on it, selling it 1993 for $350,000, a profit of $194,000. We bought and sold a few properties in between but then settled on a house at Bayview, which we acquired for $690,000. This house was in need of a lot of work. Renovations had started but the previous owner had run out of money. Again, it needed a new kitchen, two new bathrooms and extensive groundworks. After over 10 years and nearly $350,000 in renovation costs, we completed it. We eventually sold it in about 2010 for $1,800,000. A profit of over $750,000. All tax free.

We had a neighbour in Belrose who was the local butcher. His business did not make much money, but he was able to accumulate wealth by doing the exact same thing. Every two years, he would buy and sell, renovating for a profit each time. He effectively ratcheted himself up using these gains to buy bigger and better homes that became debt free due to the profits he made. All gains made were tax free because on all occasions, each house was his sole and principal residence. On this point be careful about intention. If the sole intention is somewhere to live and ancillary to this is making a profit on any future sale, then you will not run foul of the 'flipping' rules.

I know they require work. I know, for some, the thought of renovating where you live is uncomfortable and inconvenient. Unfortunately, it can also sometimes be disruptive and mean sacrifice for your family when you are constantly doing renovations. But as noted above, the rewards can be high and because the gains are tax free, they are even better.

On the sole and principal residence exemptions, be careful that you do not lose this exemption. You can only have **one** sole and principal residence at any point in time. Holiday homes or weekenders do not qualify. If you own more than one property, you need to select which property will be treated as your sole and principal residence. If any of the below exemptions apply, you

67

must make this choice in the income year you first sell one of these properties.

The capital gain on the sale of your sole and principal residence will be exempt and hence tax free if you are an Australian resident and the property:

- has been the home of you, your partner and other dependants for the whole period you have owned it
- has not been used to produce income – that is, you have not run a business from it, rented it out or purchased it with the intention to renovate and sell at a profit (or to 'flip it')
- is on land of two hectares or less.

There are some exemptions that can apply to the above depending on your situation:

- If you move into a new house – your new home is generally exempt from CGT from the time you acquire it, and your former home may also be exempt while you move.
- If you move out of your home – you can treat your former home as your main residence even if you rent it out (according to the 'six-year rule'). These rules are complicated and there is a six-month duplication period.
- If you use your home for rental purposes or to run a business, you will not receive the full main residence exemption and may need to obtain a valuation to calculate the home's market value at the time you first used it for business purposes. If you don't, you can use a 'days apportionment' rule.
- If you live in a different home to your spouse or children, you need to identify which home will be your main residence.
- If you build or renovate your home on land you own, you can treat the land as your main residence for up to four

years before you move in, provided you move in as soon as practicable after it is finished.

- If you lose your home because it is destroyed or compulsorily acquired, generally the main residence exemption will still apply.
- If your home is on more than two hectares of land, only two hectares can be CGT exempt. Again this will call for a valuation of the exempt and non-exempt portions.

By ensuring you comply with the above, no capital gains tax will be payable on your sole and principal residence when you sell it. Also, you will ignore any capital losses, meaning it cannot be offset against any capital gains on investment properties sold.

As stated above, your sole and principal residence exemption will be lost if you do any of the following:

- You rent out the property for a period of time. The rules on this vary, but basically, the capital gain is apportioned over the number of days as a rental property and sole and principal residence.
- You leave Australia and become a non-resident of Australia. In this case, any capital gains will be subject to tax, and you lose the tax-free period that the sole and principal residence was used as a home. This is a very harsh and unfair back-dating.
- The property is used for business purposes. Again, an apportionment rule will apply to tax that portion of your home as being subject to capital gains for the period it was used for business purposes.

If you are contemplating any of the above, be very careful to obtain professional help. These rules are tricky and onerous. In some cases, you will need to obtain a valuation when there is a change in use. This will set the new cost base for capital gains purposes.

I have seen many cases where what might logically seem like the case is actually not. For example, you have a home in Australia for a long period of time and then take a job overseas. Logic dictates that the period of ownership while living in Australia should be tax free, but it is not. I have seen taxpayers caught with massive capital gains tax that could have been avoided had they had better advice.

Sole and Principal Residence Rules When You Die

In an unusual twist, there is a concession that many people are not aware of. Unfortunately, it is a concession that only applies to your estate when you die. If you own a rental property and you sell it, you will be subject to capital gains tax (CGT). This also applies to your estate if you die – CGT will be payable by the estate. If, however, you move into the rental property and it becomes your sole and principal residence (does not earn income) just before you die, the property will be treated as your sole and principal residence for the entire time you have owned it. This concession applies to property inherited after 20 August 1996 for taxpayers who were a resident of Australia.

If you have inherited property in this way, note that the property will be exempt provided it is sold under a contract that settles within two years of the deceased's death. It does not matter if you rent the property or use it as your own sole and principal residence during this two-year period. You can also extend the two-year period if you need to delay the disposal due to exceptional circumstances outside your control.

This is an important concession and something to consider where elderly parents own a number of properties and wish to leave a legacy to their family in the most tax-efficient manner.

14

Tax Tip 2: Rental Properties

Most would be familiar with rental properties, but many do not fully understand the rules and concessions available. There are two situations that need to be covered. Firstly, the tax tips and tax benefits associated with the holding of rental properties. The second relates to the concessions available on their sale.

Holding Investment Property – The Tax Concessions

These fall into two broad areas, which I will clearly describe. The first is the negative gearing aspect. This is where the holding costs exceed the rental income. The second is the non-cash effect of depreciation claims, both of which have a very positive effect on the tax you pay.

Assume your annual rent from your property is $25,000 p.a. Then assume that during the year, you incur interest costs, rates, body corporate fees and some repairs that total, say, $27,000. Your net cash loss is $2000 p.a. No big deal and easy to cover. But here is where it gets interesting. If you purchased a new or relatively new property, you could expect to claim depreciation write-offs. Let's assume this is about $8000. Now your loss for tax purposes is $10,000. If you are at the top marginal tax bracket, this will give rise to a tax refund of $4700. The tax refund has more than paid the cash flow shortfall. This formula holds true for all rental properties held. Hence, you can see why professionals such as doctors, lawyers and even accountants own multiple properties – sometimes 10 or more. They are using their rental properties to reduce their current tax and build wealth for the future. Of course, wealth is only built when the properties go up in value. Over time, this is generally true. I personally have a preference for new units, as there is no maintenance, depreciation is higher and the management of the tenants can be handled by onsite managers. This is a personal preference, so you decide what is right for you.

The other point that can be useful, which is mentioned later, is that holding property can assist with one-off tax planning. Assume, in a year, that you have a large capital gain or a large income for some reason that may not reoccur. This gain (and the tax associated with it) can be offset or completely eliminated by simply prepaying one year's interest on one of your property loans. On 29 June, you borrow and pay in advance the next year's interest on a loan associated with your income-earning properties. This will be deductible in the year it is paid. Your tax bill can be reduced accordingly. I have personally done this a number of times.

Just a point on interest and tax deductibility, which I have seen clients get wrong.

The rule is that a tax deduction is based on what the money is used for, rather than the security used to obtain the loan. I had a client that repaid his rental property loan and then did a redraw to upgrade the house he lived in. The bank security was on the rental property, but the money was used for his personal residence. The client thought he was being clever, but he didn't talk to me first. He felt the above was logical, which it sort of was, but the fact is the interest was not tax deductible.

It pays to repay any non-deductible loans first and retain the tax-deductible loans. In respect of redraws, if, for example, the money is used to renovate the rental property kitchen or build a pool in the rental property, then the interest will be tax deductible. Just be careful with this one.

Tax Concessions on the Sale of Rental Property

The ATO allows a 50 per cent CGT exemption for any gains made on the sale of a rental property held for more than 12 months. This holding rule time period applies from the date a contract becomes unconditional. For example, if you purchase a property on the 1 June with a 28-day finance clause. In 14 days, your loan is approved and you advise the vendor. The date of purchase for CGT purposes will be 15 June. The same applies on the sale. The date will be when the contract to the buyer becomes unconditional. The 12-month holding rules are based on these dates. I have seen many cases where the client thought the settlement dates for the purchase and sale were used to ascertain whether the property was held for 12 months. While this may sound logical, as ownership is based on settlement, this is not the case from a tax perspective. If you have not held a rental property for in excess of 12 months, you do not get the 50 per cent CGT discount.

Consider the following example, assuming the holding rule has been satisfied:

Figure 8 Example of Tax Payable

Sale price of property	$750,000
Less agent's commission and advertising costs	$18,500
Less legal fees on the sale	$2500
Net sale proceeds	$729,000
Cost of property	$500,000
Legal fees, stamp duty, etc.	$35,000
Renovations and improvements	$85,000
Total cost of property	$620,000
Net profit	$109,000
Less 50% CGT exemption	$54,500
Taxable capital gain	$54,500

You have made $109,000 in profit. Now comes the tricky part. From the above, we have a taxable capital gain (of $54,500) that is added to your taxable income and taxed at your marginal tax rates. The following various scenarios will apply to this gain. If you plan your affairs, you should be able to choose the scenario that has the lowest tax option:

- If the property is owned in both your and your spouse's name, then only $27,250 will be added to each of your taxable income for the year.
- If you limit your income in the year the gain is made, the marginal tax will be lower. For example, if $27,250 is the only income both yourself and your spouse will earn in a year, the tax will be $1720 × 2 = $3440. If the profit is earned by one person, the tax will be $8180.
- If you are operating your business (hence your other income) through a company, you may be able to do the above by simply reducing the salary you pay yourself in the year the capital gain is made – drawings can be treated as a complying division 7A loan.
- If the above property is owned by a company, which we will assume is not a base rate entity (as the income is passive rent income), then the tax payable will be at 30 per cent on $109,000, which is a total of $32,700. Companies do not get the 50 per cent CGT discount. **This is a very important tax planning tip. Don't own real estate in a company structure.**
- If you own other assets that have unrealised capital losses, it may pay to realise those losses in the same year.
- If you cannot achieve any of the above, tax will be payable at the top marginal rate of 45 per cent, plus the Medicare levy of 2 per cent, totalling 47 per cent. Hence, you pay tax of $25,615.

Again, by planning and being proactive, you can limit the tax payable on the above gain. My main point is that you have made $109,000 on the above and will pay tax anywhere from $3440 to $25,615 (or $32,700 if owned in a company structure, which I never recommend).

Your after-tax profit will range from $105,560 to $83,385. Still a good result!

The 50 per cent CGT exemption on rental properties is something many investors can benefit from. As a taxpayer, you need to ensure you meet all the conditions and apply this concession to reduce your tax.

The above holds true for all assets that are purchased. Many people purchase a share portfolio using the above formula. I have seen massive gains from this, and I have seen massive losses. Shares can be more volatile in the short term, but in fact, in the long term, if you get it right, shares can increase in value more than property. Take Commonwealth Bank shares. When the company listed, the shares were less than $9.00 each. They are now in excess of $90.00 per share and yield around 6 per cent as a fully franked dividend.

It is not the purpose of this book to review various investment options, but merely to point out the tax planning tips associated with whatever strategy you choose. The main point is that you actually follow a strategy. That you are proactive in doing something about building wealth in a tax-effective way. These tips show you how this can be done and how to use the system to your advantage with property or shares. It's all totally legal and totally within the tax framework.

15

Tax Tip 3: Business Concessions

As mentioned earlier in this book, it is hard to save tax when you are an employee. Tax is deducted from your salary, and you have no tax planning options on how to deal with this. Your only option is to consider the tax tips associated with building wealth through property or share acquisition, as mentioned in an earlier chapter.

However, if you are in business, a whole new world opens to you. How do you structure the entity through which you trade and how can you ensure this is optimised? In this chapter, I want to dig deeper into your business and cover some clever tax planning tips that can help you reduce your tax and reinvest that money back into growing the business.

Firstly, consider that when a business buys assets or even another business, any costs associated with that acquisition are tax deductible. Large companies do that all the time. At Consolidated Press, we made many acquisitions (after Alan Bond gave us $600 million for Channel Nine). You need to be careful about how you structure the acquiring entity. In 2002, I was associated with a public company that acquired a sawmill. The acquisition cost was $8 million and it earned around $1.2 million p.a. I won't bore you with too much detail, but the acquisition nearly fell over when the seller realised they were faced with massive capital gains tax on the sale. We completely eliminated the tax by using the merger and demerger rules contained within the tax act. The vendor was able to retain nearly all of the $8 million as a tax-free gain.

The merger and demerger rules are not as complicated as they sound. Basically, an entity is acquired by another entity and becomes a subsidiary of the acquiring entity. Then it is reclassified as a consolidated entity, which allows assets to move freely between the various companies in the group, as they are now part of the same group. You move the asset, then demerge the vendor company. Of course, the consideration gets a little complicated. Usually in the merger process you may issue redeemable shares to the vendor as their consideration and then redeem them when the process is completed. The redemption provides the consideration to the vendor. The ATO has released a guideline called *Demergers in brief* that lists the requirements that need to be met.

Business acquisitions are a way to increase the size of your business by buying income-producing assets and using borrowed money to do so. If these acquisitions are well managed, they more than cover the costs. But more importantly, they allow some incredible interest write-offs and clever intergroup charges to move profit around. I can't say any more on this point.

Other concessions that are available for small businesses are listed below:

- Small businesses can claim 100 per cent write-off on
  the purchase of capital items used in your business (up
  to the $150,000 limit, based on the date of purchase).
  This includes items like plant and equipment and motor
  vehicles. If you do not qualify for the full write-off, assets
  purchased can be depreciated in accordance with their
  useful life, or in the case of small business entities (as
  defined by the tax act), 15 per cent in the first year and
  30 per cent thereafter. These claims should be considered.

If you know your equipment needs replacing, it pays to do so early and within the time limits associated with these concessions. The above 100 per cent or 15 per cent will apply even if the asset is acquired on 29 June.

- Superannuation is deductible when paid to the relevant superannuation fund. In respect of your staff, ensure all super is paid on time and in the financial year. If paid late, you lose the tax deduction. If paid in, say, July for your June wages, the tax deduction will apply in the later financial year. Hence, you should pay your June super on, say, 28 June to get a tax deduction in the current year. Also, in respect of super, ensure the director's super is maximised in accordance with the annual caps, being $27,500 for 2022.

- Bad debts write-off. If you are owed money and there is no likelihood of recovery, especially if the client goes into liquidation, make sure you write it off in the books before 30 June. Make a journal entry or raise a credit note before 30 June. This is an important rule to follow for bad debts. Also don't forget to claim back any GST if applicable.

- Closing stock and stock write-offs. There are liberal rules regarding how you value closing stock under the tax act. You can choose to value each and every item (hence each item differently) at the lower of net realisable value, cost or market selling price. This is an important tax planning tip. If you are writing off obsolete stock again, make sure you do so before 30 June.

- Prepayments – subject to the rules you can prepay up to 12 months in advance. Hence pay all of your 2023 rent on 30 June 2022 and get a tax deduction for the full amount paid.

- All expenses incurred in the operation of your business. The ATO uses the words 'necessarily incurred in the gaining or producing of assessable income'. These expenses include normal business expenses such as purchases, wages, contractors, staff training, and so on. The only exception is entertaining, which is specifically excluded (which is totally unfair).

Small Business CGT Exemptions

The next big concessions that apply to business are associated with the sale of the business. After all, there will always be a time when you want to sell, retire or simply do something else.

These are substantial but need to be carefully worked through; otherwise, they can be lost. I have seen some horrific examples of this. I had a client who sold rental management rights. His previous accountant tried to help and advised him on the flow of funds. In brief, he had the option to roll the gain into a new business, or if he didn't acquire a new business within two years, to claim the 50 per cent small business exemption and then roll what was left into his super fund. Doing the above would have ensured a total exemption from any tax payable on the capital gain. There were certain time periods for each step to ensure total exemption from any tax.

The client did not follow these. He didn't buy a new business and the entity that made the gain did not roll into his super fund. He instead took the money out of his company and placed it on deposit in his own name (as he said he could earn a higher interest in his own name). Then, within the two-year period, he put the money into his super fund. We reviewed the transaction knowing there could be an issue. We even obtained a second opinion. The client was faced with a massive tax bill. He chose to ignore it and went back to his previous accountant, thinking they had advised him and knew better. If he is ever audited, it will be a problem, but it's not our problem any longer. The point is that concessions are there, but you need to follow the letter of the law. If you get it wrong, you will lose them.

The following four CGT concessions are available only for small business:

- The small business 15-year exemption provides a total exemption for a capital gain on a CGT active asset if:
  - you have continuously owned the asset for at least 15 years
  - the relevant individual is 55 years old or older and retiring or is permanently incapacitated.
- The small business 50 per cent active asset reduction provides a 50 per cent reduction of a capital gain (you don't need to own it for 15 years).
- The small business retirement exemption provides an exemption for capital gains up to a lifetime limit of $500,000. If the individual is under 55 years old just before they make the choice, the amount must be paid into a complying superannuation fund or retirement savings account.
- The small business rollover allows you to defer all or part of a capital gain on a business asset for a minimum of two years. If you acquire a replacement asset or make a capital improvement to an existing asset within the period allowed, the gain is deferred until you:
  - dispose of the replacement or improved asset
  - change its use in particular ways.

In the last point, the deferred capital gain is in addition to any capital gain you make when you dispose of the replacement or improved asset.

The flow chart below is an extract from the ATO Guide to capital gains tax concessions for small business 2012–2013 page 8. It is current as of the time of writing. Hence, you can be assured that if you follow the rules, the gains will be exempt from tax:

Figure 9 Guide to Capital Gains Tax Concessions for Small Businesses

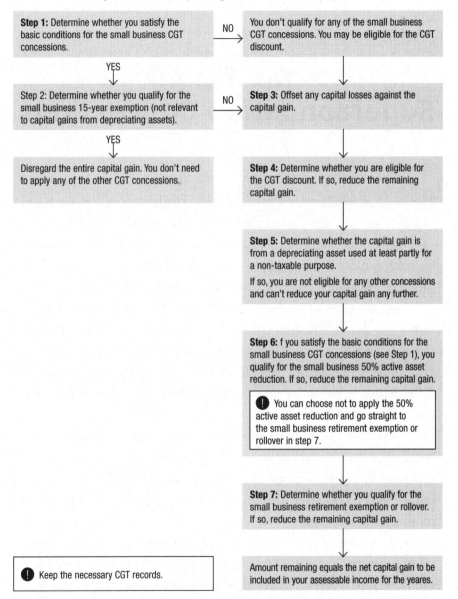

CAPITAL GAINS MADE DURING AN INCOME YEAR
You make a capital gain from a depreciating asset only to the extent you have used the depreciating asset for a non-taxable purpose.

Step 1: Determine whether you satisfy the basic conditions for the small business CGT concessions.

NO → You don't qualify for any of the small business CGT concessions. You may be eligible for the CGT discount.

YES ↓

Step 2: Determine whether you qualify for the small business 15-year exemption (not relevant to capital gains from depreciating assets).

NO → **Step 3:** Offset any capital losses against the capital gain.

YES ↓

Disregard the entire capital gain. You don't need to apply any of the other CGT concessions.

Step 4: Determine whether you are eligible for the CGT discount. If so, reduce the remaining capital gain.

Step 5: Determine whether the capital gain is from a depreciating asset used at least partly for a non-taxable purpose.

If so, you are not eligible for any other concessions and can't reduce your capital gain any further.

Step 6: f you satisfy the basic conditions for the small business CGT concessions (see Step 1), you qualify for the small business 50% active asset reduction. If so, reduce the remaining capital gain.

❗ You can choose not to apply the 50% active asset reduction and go straight to the small business retirement exemption or rollover in step 7.

Step 7: Determine whether you qualify for the small business retirement exemption or rollover. If so, reduce the remaining capital gain.

❗ Keep the necessary CGT records.

Amount remaining equals the net capital gain to be included in your assessable income for the yeares.

Source: 'ATO Guide to Capital Gains Tax Concessions for Small Business 2012–2013', p 8, https://www.ato.gov.au/uploadedFiles/Content/MEI/downloads/NAT%208384-07.pdf

16

Tax Tip 4: Superannuation Concessions

There are numerous concessions available in respect to superannuation. Firstly, of course, amounts paid into super as per the limits noted in this chapter are deductible. Secondly, superannuation is designed to be a retirement nest egg, to provide financial assistance on your future retirement.

There are two very substantial retirement exemptions that apply under the tax act to limit the tax payable on capital gains when those gains are rolled into your superannuation fund. Retirement and, hence, the ability to access your retirement money, has a different meaning under the law. It does not always mean you stop working or stop earning income.

Superannuation is your money held in a superannuation fund (either managed by you or managed by someone else) until you retire and need or want to access it to meet your retirement needs. Your money, as it grows in this environment, is taxed at 15 per cent while in accumulation mode (before you retire) or is tax free if you are retired in accordance with the definition of what retirement means.

Retirement under the tax legislation and the Superannuation Industry Supervisions Act, by definition, means meeting a condition of release. Release means being able to access your superannuation money in a tax-effective manner.

The main conditions of release are any *one* of the below:

- reaching preservation age (as defined based on your date of birth) and retiring
- reaching preservation age and commencing a transition-to-retirement income stream
- ceasing employment on or after age 60
- turning 65 (even if you haven't retired).

Provided you have reached preservation age and met one of the above conditions you will meet the retirement criteria. This is important because as soon as you meet this definition, your super account can be moved from accumulation mode into pension mode. This means all income earned by it, in relation to your member account, will be tax free. Let me repeat that: tax free.

You can also return to work and maintain both an accumulation and pension account. Clients do this constantly, as today, a person aged 60 or 65 can be fit enough to continue to work, and, in most cases, will want to do so. Especially if their superannuation balance needs a bit of topping up or they are below the balance transfer cap limit, which is currently $1.7 million (indexed).

The tax planning tip that follows this is that you can continue to contribute up to the concessional (tax-deductible) and non-concessional (non-tax-deductible) caps until the age of 75 (subject to rules on the balance transfer cap, which is currently an indexed $1.7 million). During this period, balances held in the accumulation account (on which income is taxed at 15 per cent) can effectively be rolled into a tax-free pension account at various times.

As the rules state that a pension account cannot be added to or changed, the way this is done is to roll the pension account (referred to as commute) back to accumulation. Pick up the balance currently in the accumulation account and then roll the total new accumulation balance into a new pension account. All of this is an administration action that has the effect of transferring the balance in the 15 per cent taxed accumulation account into the untaxed pension account.

We do this constantly for our clients. We roll over funds to keep the fund in either a nil tax position or the lowest tax possible. Added to this is the point that franking credits are fully refundable. Hence, it is usually the case that when the super fund tax return is lodged, there will be large tax refunds for the franking credits on any shares held. Having said the above, do not stress about the 15 per cent tax on income. It is lower than any other area. Be aware that a super fund pays 15 per cent tax on concessional (tax deductible) contributions received. It does not pay tax on non-concessional amounts paid into super.

There is also a lifetime limit on the total amount of superannuation that can be transferred into pension mode. This is called the balance transfer cap and started on 1 July 2017. For the year ended 30 June 2022, this transfer balance cap is $1.7 million and is a per member balance, not a fund balance. If your balance grows over time due to investment earnings, this will not be treated as being exceeded. However, if, through poor investments, it falls below the limits, you cannot top it up. Once exceeded and hence notionally created you cannot reverse it. Also when exceeded you can no longer contribute any further non-concessional amounts into super. It will also affect any commutations listed earlier. The rules are onerous and complicated. Hence, it pays to check what you can and cannot do with an expert in this field. Simply put, it means any excess must be placed in the accumulation account and will be taxed at 15 per cent on the pro rata portion of income that applies to this balance. This is not something to be afraid of.

As a tax tip, if a member has funds in the notional accumulation account which cannot be transferred to the pension account, you should consider whether to hold those funds inside or outside the superannuation environment. While the income on the accumulation balance is taxed at 15 per cent, it may be even more tax effective holding them personally or in an entity controlled by the family.

The final point on your pension account balance, being the amounts transferred to your retirement phase, is that to maintain this tax-free status you must draw the minimum pension amount as per the table below. This is an age-based minimum percentage that increases the older you get. You can draw any amount in excess of this amount, but you must draw the minimum. This is calculated on the 1 July balance and applies to the member's age on 1 July each year. The minimum withdrawal is also rounded to the nearest $50.00. If you do not withdraw the minimum, you will lose the tax-free status of your pension account. The amount drawn is tax free in the member's hands.

Figure 10 Minimum Pension Amount to be Withdrawn

Age	Statutory pension withdrawal	Covid-related 50% reduction for 2019, 2020, 2021, 2022 income years
Under 65	4.0%	2%
65–74	5.0%	2.5%
75–79	6.0%	3%
80–84	7.0%	3.5%
85–89	9.0%	4.5%
90–94	11.0%	5.5%
95 or more	14.0%	7%

Source: ATO website: https://www.ato.gov.au/uploadedFiles/Content/MEI/downloads/NAT%208384-07.pdf

In the 2022–23 Federal Budget, the government has announced an extension of this reduced minimum pension payment to the 2023 Income Tax Year.

Rollover of Capital Gains to Super

When you sell a business, you will not be taxed on the rolled over portion of any capital gains that you move into super There are rollover provisions in the capital gains tax legislation to allow this when you sell a business or active asset (subject to various limits).

You need to decide whether you qualify for the small business retirement exemption or rollover exemptions. If you do, you may choose the small business retirement exemption or the small business rollover for the remaining amount of capital gain if you meet the conditions. As per the case study in the previous chapter, the client decided to roll the balance of the capital gain that was taxable into his super fund. You have the option to choose both concessions for different parts of any remaining capital gain.

Small Business Retirement Exemption

You can use your small business retirement exemption to disregard all or part of a capital gain. You can choose to apply the retirement exemption to any amount of capital gain remaining after you have applied the other concessions or before any other concessions.

The amount you choose to disregard is called the exempt amount. The amount of any capital gain that exceeds the CGT exempt amount does not qualify for this exemption. The exempt amount must not exceed your CGT retirement exemption limit. There is a lifetime limit on this of $500,000. Eligible termination payments (ETPs) fall within this limit, so it pays to check if you have received any of these in previous years, as they will reduce your lifetime limit of $500,000.

If you meet the above criteria, any capital gain you make from the sale of your business, up to the above limits, will be tax free if you roll it into your super fund. If your super fund is in pension mode, as noted above, any income earned on this money will also be tax free.

As a tax tip, as you move closer to retirement age, it pays to consider transferring as many of your assets (including money) into super. Also remember there are limits that increase with age. So consider this strategy while you are able to. For example, if you have property or shares and receive a net income of, say, $100,000 in your personal name, you will pay $24,967 in tax. If this is in your super fund, no tax will be payable. A super fund can acquire from a member (you) listed shares and business real property (commercial property), hence not residential property or shares that are not listed on a stock exchange. There will be some tax planning required to transfer as many assets as possible into your super fund.

As a tip, consider:

- Maximising the concessional and non-concessional limits ($27,500 and $110,000, respectively, as of the 1 July 2021). I know many young people fail to see the benefit in putting money into super that may be locked up until age 60. But consider the compounding effect of continuous contributions. And remember it is your money. It is like placing $27,500 into a separate bank account and getting a tax deduction for doing so.
- To contribute money into super (and get a tax deduction), you must meet a work test when you reach 67. If you are younger than 67, this work test does not apply. The work test is met if you work at least 40 hours in a 30-day period in the year, but you must meet this test before you actually make the contributions. If your balance is under $300,000 you have a one-year exemption from this work test. There are plans to change or repeal the work tests.
- Using the carried forward rules for contributions and the carry back rule for non-concessional contributions, if you qualify. If your superannuation balance is less than $500,000 and you did not contribute up to the caps in

previous years, you can take advantage of the unused cap for five years and contribute extra into super. If the reverse happened and you contribute in excess of your cap, say $30,000 in 2022, you can carry the excess of $2500 to 2023. This is a five-year rolling forward rule.

- For those who have a low superannuation balance, the downsizer rules may help increase your balance in super. If you are selling your home (sole and principal residence), you can use the downsizer rules to contribute up to $300,000 (each partner) into your super. This downsizer rule is not caught under the above non-concessional caps but will count towards the transfer balance cap of $1.7 million. You can only use this rule once and the amount will be considered for determining the eligibility for the age pension. You or your spouse must have owned the property for 10 years or more and be over 65 to use this rule. The 10-year ownership period is generally calculated from the date of settlement of the purchase to the date of settlement of the sale. You must also make the superannuation contribution within 90 days of receiving the sale proceeds, which will usually be the date of settlement. Importantly, you do not need to buy a smaller house, just sell a qualifying property.

- Reviewing the taxable and non-taxable components of your superannuation account to determine if a recontribution strategy will work to convert the taxable amounts into non-taxable components. In a superannuation fund, tax-deductible contribution (concessional amounts) will be in what is called a notional taxable account. This means that if you die and the balance is paid out to a non-dependant beneficiary, it will be taxed at 15 per cent. To avoid this, consider withdrawing the taxable components and re-contribute the money back into super as non-concessional contributions (up to the non-concessional cap). To do this, you need to obtain professional advice as there can be restrictions.

Imagine the following very simplistic scenario. On retirement, you and your spouse each have $1.2 million in your super fund, earning about a 6 per cent return. The fund would make $144,000 each year in income. No tax would be payable on this income. You would both be able to draw $72,000 in income, which again would be tax free in your hands. If you purchased, say, 10,000 Afterpay shares at $1.00 that increased to $100.00 per share and made $1 million in profit, this would also be tax free if in super. If you needed extra money, you can draw any amount you like (up to the balance of your account, of course), which would also be tax free.

So when I say superannuation is a tax haven, you can see in the above example how this is the case. Yes, the rules are complicated and onerous. But that should not frighten you.

17

Tax Tip 5: Gearing

In the chapter on rental properties and using these as a method to reduce tax, I covered the deductibility of interest on loans. This is a way to use bank money to make more money and use the tax deductibility of the interest to help reduce your tax.

Let me be clear: the investment you consider purchasing must stack up. You do not enter into a loan for tax reasons only. You do not spend a dollar to save 45 cents. That would not make sense. But you would if you knew that the one-dollar expenditure would earn you a return of, say, 15 per cent and, in time, be worth two dollars. That would make economic sense. For the purpose of this exercise, I will cover the tax aspects, noting that the above is a given and that the investment must make economic sense. You can buy a business, rental property, share portfolio or commercial investment, the formula holds true no matter what the underlying asset is.

Let's assume you purchase an asset for $1 million that you know is undervalued and that you can make money on. Let's also assume it is an income-producing asset but, at this stage, it will take a year or two to generate income. If you borrowed 100 per cent on the purchase price at 6 per cent interest, you have an immediate write-off of $60,000. If you have income from other areas, then this $60,000 write-off (interest only) could be worth $28,200 in reduced tax or as a tax refund. Assume you capitalise the interest, which means you do not pay it, but add it to the loan, as banks will often allow this. On some loans, they will even allow you to borrow the first year's interest in advance. Doing this with an asset that increases in value means you make a large profit and reduce your tax, all with no actual cash outlay.

Taking this further, if you acquired the above asset on the 29 June, you would receive a tax windfall of $28,200. Of course, the asset must stack up and eventually you will need to repay the loan and the interest accrued. But my point is, you are using a great asset purchase in a tax-effective way to yield some big upfront benefits.

We had an engineering client with a large bill due to some one-off projects. He purchased, fully geared on the 29 June, a parcel of NAB shares for around $500,000. Interest was paid in advance. This totally eliminated his tax bill. He told me later it created an interesting problem. Over the next year, the shares went up 50 per cent, which created a tax issue, but a nice one. He made $250,000, which would more than cover any tax payable thereon. The shares were hedged, so if they went down, he did not lose. It would just have cost him the interest and hedging costs.

Public companies do this all the time. They acquire companies or businesses and borrow the money in order to get a massive write-off. The tax saved often goes a long way towards the growth of their business base and share price. Again, providing the investment is a good investment, growth is key to building wealth. The tax refund can be a key factor in making that happen. Then, when you grow the business, you avail yourself of the associated CGT concessions when you ultimately sell. You win both ways.

My point is to be lateral in your thinking. Use the system to leverage your investment to increase your yield and also receive other benefits, like a big tax windfall or tax saving.

18

Tax Tip 6: Asset Write-offs

Earlier in this book, I covered the massive tax stimulus that the government provided to small businesses during the Covid-19 pandemic. One of these is the asset write-off rules, designed to stimulate investment. Generally, in business, you can write off the cost of an asset used in your business over its useful life. This is known as depreciation. For small business entities, they have the option of pooling their assets and claiming 15 per cent in the first year and 30 per cent thereafter. They may choose not to do this but instead use a useful life method and write off their capital purchases over the effective life of the asset. Be aware that in some cases you do not have a choice.

As an important tax tip, if you purchase an asset (and it is received, installed and ready for use) on, for example, 29 June in any year, you can claim 15 per cent of the asset value even though you have only owned that asset for one day.

There is also a low value pool for assets costing less than $300.00. These can be written off in full.

I must stress the pooling, the small business test and simplified depreciation rules when joined with the tax stimulus measures and full expensing rules to allow 100 per cent write-off are a minefield. Measure upon measure were introduced each with different rules.

In some cases they overlap, in others they do not. Ensure you review the table listed at Figure 11, 'Interaction of Tax Depreciation Incentives' on page 98.

Part of the tax stimulus measure was continual expansions of the instant asset – write-offs for eligible businesses. Hence, an eligible business can claim an immediate deduction for the business portion of the cost of an asset in the year the asset is first used or installed ready for use.

Instant asset write-off can be used for:

- multiple assets, if the cost of each individual asset is less than the relevant threshold
- new and second-hand assets.

If you are a small business, you will need to apply the simplified depreciation rules in order to claim the instant asset write-off. It cannot be used for assets that are excluded from those rules.

This eligibility and correct threshold amount depends on when the asset was purchased, first used or installed ready for use.

Motor Vehicles

To add to complexity, some special rules apply to motor vehicles. A motor vehicle cost limit applies to passenger vehicles (except a motorcycle or similar vehicle) designed to carry a load less than one tonne and less than nine passengers.

The cost limit is:

- $59,136 for the 2020–2021 income year
- $60,733 for the 2021–2022 income year.

The one tonne load capacity is the maximum load a vehicle can carry. It is also known as the payload capacity. This is defined as the gross vehicle mass (GVM) as specified on the compliance plate by the manufacturer, reduced by the basic kerb weight of the vehicle. To add more definition to this, the basic kerb weight is the weight of the vehicle with a full tank of fuel, oil and coolant together with spare wheel, tools (including jack) and factory-installed options. It does not include the weight of passengers, goods or accessories. Hence, the payload capacity = GVM – basic kerb weight.

The above car limit does not apply to vehicles modified for use by people with a disability.

You cannot claim this excess cost over the car limit under any other depreciation rules. To add more complication to this, if you are registered for GST you can only claim the ex-GST portion of the above that is over the car limit. Hence, if you purchase a vehicle for $60,000, the ex-GST portion is $54,545. As it is below the car limit, this is the amount you can claim.

The instant asset write-off is limited to the business portion of the car limit for the relevant income tax year. For example, the car limit is $60,733 for the 2021–2022 income tax year. If you use your vehicle for 75 per cent business use, the total you can claim under the instant asset write-off is 75 per cent of $60,733, which equals $45,550.

Where the Cost is Higher than the Cost-limit Threshold

As stated earlier, if you are a small business (as defined), you must use the simplified depreciation rules to claim the instant asset write-off. If you use the simplified depreciation rules and the cost of the asset is the same as or more than the relevant instant asset write-off threshold, the asset must be placed into the small business pool mentioned earlier.

- For assets you start to hold, and first use (or have installed ready for use) for a taxable purpose from 7.30 pm (AEDT) on 6 October 2020 to 30 June 2022, the instant asset write-off threshold does not apply. You can immediately deduct the business portion of the asset under temporary full expensing.
- For income years ending between 6 October 2020 and 30 June 2022, you can deduct the balance of your small business pool under temporary full expensing.

If you are not using the simplified depreciation rules (because you are not a small business or have chosen not to apply the rules), you work out how much you can deduct under the temporary full expensing or the 'backing business investment – accelerated deprecation' rules, if you meet the eligibility criteria for those rules. Otherwise, you apply the general depreciation rules.

How Much Do You Claim?

If you receive a trade-in, this must be added back to the amount paid in calculating the relevant threshold. This is the threshold for the car limits, full tax expensing and all other thresholds mentioned in this chapter. GST must be deducted from the costs of the asset, if you are registered for GST. If you are not registered for GST, the threshold is the GST-inclusive amount.

To calculate the amount you can claim, you must subtract any private use portion. The balance (that is the portion you use to earn assessable income) is generally the taxable purpose portion (business purpose portion).

In an unfair twist, while you can only claim the taxable purpose portion as a tax deduction, the entire cost of the asset must be less than the relevant thresholds mentioned above.

What are Eligible Businesses?

Eligibility to use instant asset write-off on an asset depends on:

- your aggregated turnover (the total ordinary income of your business and that of any associated businesses)
- the date you purchased the asset
- when it was first used or installed ready for use
- the cost of the asset being less than the threshold.

You are not eligible to use instant asset write-off on an asset if your aggregated turnover is $500 million or more.

If temporary full expensing applies to the asset, you do not apply the instant asset write-off.

The Interaction of Tax Depreciation and Incentives

Again the government has overcomplicated this due to the changes made over the past two years and a continuous extension, refinement and changing of the rules. The following tables are from the ATO website.

They are confusing but it is simply too hard to define this in a simpler way:

Figure 11 Interaction of Tax Depreciation Incentives

Temporary Full Expensing	Instant Asset Write-Off – to 11 March 2020	Instant Asset Write-Off – from 12 March 2020	Backing Business Investment
Allows full write-off for eligible assets first held at or after Budget Time 6 October 2020. 'Temporary' means it does not apply to assets first used or installed for taxable purposes after 30 June 2022. As part of the Budget 2021–22, temporary full expensing is to be extended for another year, though at time of writing, the measures announced as part of the Budget were not yet law.	Allows full write-off for eligible assets costing less than $30,000 if first acquired at or after Budget Time 2 April 2019 (or Budget Time 12 May 2015 for small business entities using simplified depreciation). Assets must have been first used or installed for a taxable purpose between 2 April 2019 and 11 March 2020.	Allows full write-off for eligible assets costing less than $150,000 if first acquired at or after Budget Time 2 April 2019 (or Budget Time 12 May 2015 for small business entities using simplified depreciation) and on or before 31 December 2020. Assets must have been first used or installed for a taxable purpose between 12 March 2020 and 30 June 2021.	Allows for an accelerated depreciation of eligible assets first held and first used or installed for a taxable purpose between 12 March 2020 and 30 June 2021.

Source: ATO website, https://www.ato.gov.au/uploadedFiles/Content/SME/downloads/Interaction_of_ tax_depreciation_incentives.pdf

Tax Write-off Thresholds

There have been so many changes over the last couple of years that it is important to check the dates and rules. The following table contains all the rules.

Figure 12 Instant Asset Write-off Thresholds for Small Businesses that Apply the Simplified Depreciation Rules

Eligible businesses	Date range for when asset first used or installed ready for use	Threshold
Less than $10 million aggregated turnover	12 March 2020 to 30 June 2021, providing the asset is purchased by 31 December 2020	$150,000
Less than $10 million aggregated turnover	7.30 pm (AEDT) on the 2 April 2019 to 11 March 2020	$30,000
Less than $10 million aggregated turnover	29 January 2019 to prior to 7.30 pm (AEDT) on 2 April 2019	$25,000
Less than $10 million aggregated turnover	1 July 2016 to 28 January 2019	$20,000
Less than $2 million aggregated turnover	7.30 pm (AEST) on 12 May 2015 to 30 June 2016	$20,000
Less than $2 million aggregated turnover	1 January 2014 to prior to 7.30 pm (AEST) 12 May 2015	$1000
Less than $2 million aggregated turnover	1 July 2012 to 31 December 2013	$6500
Less than $2 million aggregated turnover	1 July 2011 to 30 June 2012	$1000

Source: ATO Instant asset write-off for eligible businesses, https://www.ato.gov.au/Business/Depreciation-and-capital-expenses-and-allowances/Simpler-depreciation-for-small-business/Instant-asset-write-off/?=redirected_instantassetwriteoff

Temporary Full Expensing – Recent Changes

The government introduced a 'Temporary full expensing' rule to support businesses and encourage investment. An eligible business can claim an immediate deduction for the business portion of the cost of an asset in the year it is first used or installed ready for use for a taxable purpose. This overrides the existing legislation and hence the government released the Law Companion Guide (LCR 2021/3) to cover how this will work.

For assets first used or installed ready for use between 12 March 2020 until the 30 June 2021, and purchased by the 31 December 2020, the instant asset write-off:

- threshold amount for each asset is $150,000 (up from $30,000)
- eligibility extends to businesses with an aggregated turnover of less than $500 million (up from $50 million).

From 7.30 pm (AEDT) on the 6 October 2020 until the 30 June 2022, temporary full expensing allows a deduction for:

- the business portion of the cost of new eligible depreciating assets for businesses with an aggregated turnover under $5 billion or for corporate tax entities that satisfy the alternative test
- the business portion of the cost of eligible second-hand assets for businesses with an aggregated turnover under $50 million
- the balance of a small business pool at the end of each income year in this period for businesses with an aggregated turnover under $10 million.

The above does not apply to improvements to property or other assets, like replacing a roof with a better roof, or new concrete floors in chicken sheds. It only covers plant and equipment.

Hence, for the above 'temporary full expenses' rules, the instant asset write-off threshold does not apply. You can immediately deduct the business portion of the asset's cost under temporary full expensing.

For the 2020–2021 and 2021–2022 income years, an eligible entity can claim in its tax return a deduction for the business portion of the cost of:

- eligible new assets first held, first used or installed ready for use for a taxable purpose between 7.30 pm (AEDT) on 6 October 2020 and 30 June 2022

- eligible second-hand assets where both
  - the asset was first held, first used or installed ready for use for a taxable purpose between 7.30 pm (AEDT) on 6 October 2020 and 30 June 2022
  - the eligible entity's aggregated turnover is less than $50 million
- improvements incurred between 7.30 pm (AEDT) on 6 October 2020 and 30 June 2022 to
  - eligible assets
  - existing assets that would be eligible assets except that they are held before 7.30 pm (AEDT) on 6 October 2020
- eligible assets of small business entities using the simplified depreciation rules and the balance of their small business pool.

Fortunately, you can make a choice to opt out of temporary full expensing for an income year on an asset-by-asset basis if you are not using the simplified depreciation rules. You must advise the ATO of your choice to opt out either in your tax return or by the day you lodge your tax return for the income year to which the choice relates.

In working through the above, we have needed to use this opt-out provision as, in some cases, the full expensing was of no value, or even cost the company more This is particularly the case where we wanted to use the loss carry back rules mentioned next.

If you are contemplating full expensing and this will create a loss, you need to consider if you have received any foreign tax credits, franking credits from shares or had withholding tax deducted that you now wish to claim back. The above can only be offset to Australian tax and cannot be carried forward. Hence, if you do not show a profit with tax payable that will be reduced by any of the above, these credits will be lost. Franking credits can be converted into a tax loss and carried forward to a subsequent tax year. But foreign tax credits, and overseas withholding tax will be lost forever.

Loss Carry-back Rules

A business may make a trading tax loss in a year. It may also show a tax loss in an income year due to claiming an immediate deduction under temporary full expensing rules. If the business is a corporate entity, it can choose to either:

- carry the tax loss forward and use it to offset any future income; or
- if in the 2019 tax year, tax was paid, the company may be eligible for a refundable tax offset under loss carry back rules.

Loss carry back rules provide a refundable tax offset that eligible corporate entities can claim after the end of their 2020–2021 and/ or 2021–2022 income years in their company tax returns.

It means that if a company paid tax in the 2019 tax year, the 2021 or 2022 tax loss can be carried back to effectively gain a refund of this tax previously paid.

19

Tax Tip 7: Share Portfolios

In this section, I have covered many of the tax tips associated with buying and selling assets. In this chapter, I want to be specific about shares and share portfolios. As each situation can vary dramatically, you should always seek professional help if they apply to you. There are some specific rules that apply to shares that you need to be aware of. Some of these apply to all asset classes, some do not (and, of course, legislation and case law can change the rules):

- Whether you are carrying on a business as a share trader or as a share investor.
- Gearing, and when you can claim it.
- Eligibility for 50 per cent CGT exemption, provided you hold a share for 12 months.
- The 90-day holding rule for imputation credits, and how you can lose them.
- Part IVA of the *Income Tax Assessment Act 1936* that sets out rules on crystalising losses and gains for tax reasons only, also known as the 'wash' rule (see page 111).

The tax treatment of shares depends on whether you're considered to be holding shares as an investor or carrying on a business as a share trader.

In tax (and accounting), there are two terms: capital account or revenue account. An investor incurs expenses that are on capital account, whereas a trader incurs expenses on revenue account. This affects whether certain costs are accumulated and claimed as part of the cost base (for CGT sales purposes) or are deducted immediately if you are carrying on a business. If you are a share trader, interest, gains and losses are all taxable/deductible in a year, regardless of whether you have actually sold the shares. A little like trading stock.

This is a complicated area, so it's worth considering how the rules apply to you and how you might like those to apply to give you the lowest tax position.

What is a Share Investor?

To be classified as a share investor (as distinct from carrying on the business of share trading), the intention must be that the shares are purchased and held for the purpose of earning income from dividends and similar receipts. The tax effect is that:

- the cost of purchase of shares is not an allowable deduction against current-year income but is a capital cost (and CGT discount if you qualify) and subject to tax when sold
- receipts from the sale of shares are not assessable income, but any capital gain on the shares is subject to capital gains tax
- a net capital loss from the sale of shares can't be offset against (ordinary) income from other sources but can be offset against another capital gains or carried forward to offset against future capital gains
- the transaction costs of buying or selling shares is not an allowable deduction against income, forms part of

the cost base of the shares and is taken into account in determining the amount of any capital gain
- dividends and other similar receipts from the shares are included in assessable income
- costs (such as interest on borrowed money) incurred in earning dividend income are an allowable deduction against current year income.

Share Trading as Business

A person is deemed to be a share trader if they carry out their business for the purpose of earning income from buying and selling shares. Hence, the tax position for a share trader is that:

- receipts from the sale of shares constitute assessable income
- shares purchased are regarded as trading stock
- costs incurred in buying or selling shares, including the cost of the shares, are an allowable deduction in the year in which they are incurred
- shares held on 30 June are treated as closing stock and valued in accordance with the trading stock rules at the lower of cost or net realisable value. A determination can be made for every share held based on any or either of the above closing stock rules. Closing stock in one year is opening stock in the following year
- dividends and other similar receipts are included in assessable income
- costs (such as interest on borrowed money) incurred in earning income are an allowable deduction against current year income.

How do you Decide Whether You're Carrying on a Business of Share Trading or Simply Holding Shares for Investment Purposes?

The rules on whether or not you're carrying on a business of share trading are the same rules that apply to any other undertaking for tax purposes. Under the tax law, a 'business' includes 'any profession, trade, employment, vocation or calling, but does not include occupation as an employee'. The question of whether a person is a share trader or a long-term share investor has been determined by case law. Everyone's situation can be different, hence sometimes this can be difficult to be certain which way the ATO will treat your activities. You can seek a private ruling to clarify this. Often taxpayers challenge the ATO and the court position and hence many rulings and determinations have been made on this point alone. These rulings are centred around the following four areas, which are explained in detail. It is a very important distinction and care must be taken should you choose to adopt a particular path (in the business of share trading or as a share investor):

- The nature of the activities, particularly whether they have the purpose of profit making.
- The repetition, volume and regularity of the activities, and the similarity to other businesses in your industry.
- Organisation in a business-like way, including keeping accounts and records of trading stock, business premises, licences or qualifications, a registered business name and an ABN.
- The amount of capital invested.

Nature of Activity and Purpose of Profit Making

We all enter into a business transaction to make a profit. However, sometimes the circumstances work against us, and this is not the case. We often see situations where a loss has been made and the person now seeks to claim those losses as trading losses, especially if they want to offset these losses against other income like salary income. If they made a gain, they may try to say they are an investor and, hence, will not need to declare the gains until the shares are sold.

The intention to make a profit is not, on its own, sufficient to establish that a business is being carried on. A share trader is an entity or person who carries out business activities for the purpose of earning income from buying and selling shares. Shares may be held for either investment or trading purposes, and profits on sale are earned in either case. A person who invests in shares as an investor (rather than a share trader) does so with the intention of earning income from dividends and receipts but is not carrying on business activities. It is necessary for you to consider not only your intention to make a profit, but also the facts of your situation. This includes details of how the activity has actually been carried out or a business plan of how the activities will be conducted.

A business plan might show, for example:

- an analysis of each potential investment
- analysis of the current market
- research to show when or where a profit may arise
- the basis of your decision-making on when to hold or sell shares.

Repetition, Volume and Regularity

Repetition – that is, the frequency of transactions or the number of similar transactions – is a significant characteristic of business activities. The higher the volume of your purchases and sales of shares, the more likely it is that you are carrying on a business. A business of share trading could also be expected to involve the purchase of shares on a regular basis through a regular or routine method.

Acting in a Business-like Way and Keeping Records

A person conducting a share trading business could reasonably be expected to be involved in the study of daily and longer-term trends, analysis of a company's prospectus and annual reports, and seeking advice from experts. Your qualifications, expertise, training or skills in this area are relevant to determining whether your activities constitute a business. Failure to keep records of purchases and sales of shares would make it difficult for a taxpayer to establish that a business of share trading was being carried on.

Amount of Capital Invested

The amount of capital that you invest in buying shares is not considered to be a crucial factor in determining whether you are carrying on a business of share trading. This is an area in which it is possible to carry out business activities with a relatively small amount of capital. Conversely, you may also invest a substantial amount of capital and not be considered to be a share trader.

Let me illustrate the above with two examples from our client base.

Case Study 1 – A Share Investor

Mrs G has been buying shares for 30 years. She rarely sells any shares and has amassed a portfolio of some 20 stocks that have a cost base of around $2 million and a market value of $7 million. She lives off the dividends, which are now around $300,000 per year. She is treated as a share investor (not a trader). She only pays tax on shares when sold and is able to avail herself of any capital gains tax discounts on the sale.

Case Study 2 – A Share Trader

Mr N logs on every day to the share market. His computer has three screens, and he actively watches all movements. In a day, he might buy and sell the same stock, he might open positions with CFD (contracts for difference) to short sell or buy. At the end of the year, all shares held are treated as closing stock. Gains or losses during the year will be taxable or deductible. All unrealised gains will be taxable, and all unrealised losses will be deductible. The cost of running his office and all costs associated with his business are deductible. He is active in the mining sector. In doing his research, he sometimes visits those mines. All of these costs will also be deductible.

In summary, the advantages of carrying on a business as a share trader include:

- Share traders can offset any trading losses incurred over the financial year against other assessable income.
- Costs incurred in buying or selling shares are an allowable deduction in the year in which they are incurred.
- All costs associated with running the business will be deductible.

The bad news is that they can't take advantage of the 50 per cent capital gains discount on shares held for more than 12 months.

The best way of looking at it is that share traders buy and sell shares for profit, whereas share investors buy shares to hold as an investment. In the same vein as other businesses, any profits made by the share trader are regarded as assessable income, and all costs incurred in running the business are deductible.

Gearing and Loans Associated with Buying Shares

While the determination on whether you are a share investor or carrying on the business of share investment affects many deductions, it does not affect claiming a tax deduction for interest paid to purchase shares. They must be shares that will or are likely to pay a dividend. This is because both a share investor or a share trader will incur these costs. The tax tip on this is that by using gearing, you are able to both multiply gains, but it will also multiply losses. Gearing has tax advantages and also you can use the prepayment rules to maximise your tax deductions. As a rule, it is usually prudent to only gear around 30 per cent of any share portfolio due to the inherent volatility of shares. Hence, with gearing, $70,000 cash and a $30,000 bank loan allow $100,000 to be invested into the share market. The same rules apply to rental property. This will be a personal decision. I have seen many clients gear 100 per cent on blue chip shares and come out in front. I have seen others lose substantial sums. Be careful and seek advice. Share trading is not for the faint-hearted. We had one client who boasted about his share trading skills. He lost $7 million over a 10-year period.

Limiting Rules – Ability to Receive a Franking Credit Refund

Your entitlement to a franking credit may be affected by the holding period rule, the related payments rule or the dividend washing integrity rule (mentioned below). The general effect of the holding period rule and the related payments rule is that even if a dividend is accompanied by a dividend statement advising that there is a franking credit attached to the dividend, you are not entitled to claim the franking credit. The entitlement to a franking credit can also be affected if you enter into a scheme with the dominant purpose of obtaining franking credits (referred to as franking credit trading).

Holding Period Rule

The holding period rule requires you to continuously hold shares 'at risk' for at least 45 days (90 days for certain preference shares) to be eligible for the franking credit. However, under the small shareholder exemption, this rule does not apply if your total franking credit entitlement is below $5000. This is roughly equivalent to receiving a fully franked dividend of:

- $11,666 (for companies that are not base rate entities, with a corporate tax rate of 30 per cent); or
- $13,181 (for companies that are base rate entities, with a corporate tax rate of 27.5 per cent).

This means that you must continuously own shares 'at risk' for at least 45 days (90 days for certain preference shares), not counting the day of acquisition or disposal, to be eligible for any franking credit. The financial risk of owning shares may be reduced through arrangements such as hedges, options and futures.

If you acquire shares, or an interest in shares, and you have not already satisfied the holding period rule before the day on which the shares become ex-dividend, the holding period rule commences on the day after the day on which you acquired the shares or interest. The shares become ex-dividend on the day after the last day on which acquisition of the shares will entitle you to receive the dividend. You must then hold the shares or interest (at risk) for 45 days (90 days for certain preference shares), excluding the day of disposal. For each of these days, you must have 30 per cent or more of the ordinary financial risks of loss and opportunities for gain from owning the shares or interest.

You have to satisfy the holding period rule once only for each purchase of shares. You are then entitled to the franking credits attached to those shares, unless the related payments rule applies.

The Wash Rule – Affecting Profits and Losses on Sale of Shares

It is common, if you have made a substantial gain on the sale of shares, and you are also holding shares that have decreased in value to consider selling them to offset the gains made on other shares. However, the ATO is aware of this strategy, and while it is difficult to prove, you need to be aware that it is possible to do so, even if unintentionally done. If, for instance, you sold some loss-making shares on the 30 June and bought them back on the 1 July, that would clearly show intention. The ATO has issued tax ruling TR 2008/1, also known as 'Income tax: application of Part IVA' of the *Income Tax Assessment Act 1936*, to 'wash sale' arrangements. The effect will be to deny the loss being claimed as an offset against the capital gain.

Be mindful that this rule exists and be careful with how any such transaction is conducted.

The above rules are complicated, so you need to be careful that you comply with them. This will ensure any gains, franking credits or any issues associated with building wealth through the acquisition of shares are complied with. Most are reasonably easy to comply with if you are aware that they exist and take measures to ensure you do not inadvertently do something to cause the loss of the concession. If you are unsure, seek professional help.

Employee Share Schemes

In the 2022–23 Federal Budget, the government announced an expansion of the Employee Share Scheme (ESS). This allows a company to issue shares or rights to employees as part of their employment. It allows the employees to share in the profitability and growth of the business. The new measures are designed to expand access to these schemes, especially ahead of any intended float. Each participant can access up to $30,000 per year in either options or shares for up to five years.

It is important to consider the tax implications, as ESS can have varying tax treatments and taxing points based on either the grant of the shares or options, their current market value or the CGT on their sale. These measures will be worth reviewing when the legislation is released. It tends to be easier to work backwards on this one to ascertain the best taxing point to ensure tax is minimised.

20

Tax Tip 8: Year-end Tax Planning Tips for Employees

As an employee, claiming tax deductions is difficult and requires care. This is one area the ATO focuses on. Unfortunately, over half the money the ATO collects is from salary and wage earners ($233 billion in 2021 against total collections of $451 billion; Commissioner of Taxation Annual Report 2020–21, p 67).

These tips may help you reduce your tax liability in your personal income tax return, as well as claim certain offsets that may be available to you.

The ATO collects data from various places and prefills that information into your personal file that can then be prefilled into your income tax return. Usually, it takes until the end of July for this data to find its way to your personal tax file. If service providers are slow, this can take until mid-August.

You should check your income statement from your employer to ensure it says 'tax ready' and your private health insurance, dividend and interest information is available before you prepare your tax return. Otherwise, you're potentially lodging your return with incomplete data and may need to amend your tax return or pay additional tax.

If you've used the myDeductions tool in the ATO app, you can email your data or upload it to prefill your tax return. Most tax agents, depending on their software, can access your data via the tax agent portal and upload it into their tax preparation software.

Declare Your Income

Your income statement (previously referred to as your PAYG statement) will show as 'tax ready' when your employer has finalised it. Employers need to make a final declaration by 14 July if they have 20 or more employees, or 31 July if they have 19 or fewer employees. The introduction of single-touch payroll for all employers has facilitated this process.

JobKeeper payments are treated the same as your usual salary or wages from your employer and are included in your income statement as either salary and wages or as an allowance, depending on your circumstances. JobSeeker payments that were paid by Centrelink will be available on your tax account and can be uploaded into your tax return by the end of July.

If you have received any insurance money as income protection, sickness or accident insurance payments, redundancy payments and accrued leave payments, they must be included in your tax return. Most insurance companies report this to the ATO, but not all. So be careful that you include it.

If you take leave, are temporarily stood down or lose your job and receive a payment from your employer, there are different tax rules that may apply for the different payments.

If you have received an early release payment from your superannuation due to Covid-19, you will not need to pay tax on these amounts and will not need to include these amounts in your tax return.

If you have sold assets, which may include a property, shares or other assets (including your sole and principal residence), you will need to declare this and work through the taxable/non-taxable aspects of this.

Reporting Income and Expenses from the Cash or Online Economy

If you drive people for a rideshare service, do odd jobs, rent out your home or other possessions, run social media accounts or sell products, your income from such activity may be assessable and your expenses deductible. This can include barter and cryptocurrency.

The ATO is receiving data from a range of websites, including AirTasker, Uber, AirBnb and eBay, which is matched against tax returns. Make sure you keep records and report correctly. For some activities, such as online selling, you may need to first determine whether you are in business.

Work-related Deductions

Claiming all work-related deduction entitlements may save considerable income tax. Typical work-related expenses include employment-related mobile phone, internet usage and computer repairs, as well as union fees and professional subscriptions the employee paid themselves and for which they were not reimbursed.

Be aware that the ATO continues to check work-related expense claims. The ATO expects to see a substantial increase in deductions for working from home or protective items required for work, as well as a reduction in claims for laundry expenses or travel expenses. You cannot claim the cost of travelling to and from work and working from home as a result of Covid-19.

If your usual pattern of work has changed during the year due to Covid-19 or other circumstances, you may need to complete an additional record for the period your work pattern changed, especially where claims are calculated using representative periods.

Just remember, for an expense to qualify:

- you must have spent the money yourself and weren't reimbursed

- it must directly relate to earning your income
- you must have a record to prove it.

Working from Home and Home Office Expenses

When you are an employee who regularly works from home and part of your home has been set aside primarily or exclusively for the purpose of work, a home office deduction may be allowable. Typical home office costs include heating, cooling, lighting and office equipment depreciation.

If you own your home, we do not recommend claiming fixed costs such as rates, mortgage interest, and so on. These would normally be claimed using a square metre rule. This is because that percentage of business use will affect any sole and principal residence exemptions from capital gains tax. If you rent, then you should certainly make this claim. You need to justify the business space and ensure it is not used for private purposes.

The ATO is also allowing the use of a shortcut method for working from home claims between 1 March 2020 and 30 June 2022. This enables you to claim a deduction of 80 cents per hour. You can use this method if you:

- are working from home to fulfil your employment duties and not just carrying out minimal tasks, such as occasionally checking emails or taking calls
- have incurred additional running expenses as a result of working from home.

The shortcut method doesn't require you to have a dedicated work area, such as a private study. If this method is chosen, no other expenses for working from home in that period can be claimed.

You must keep a record of the number of hours you have worked from home. This could be a timesheet, roster, diary or similar, documenting the hours you worked.

If you use the other methods, you must also keep a record of the number of hours you worked from home, along with records of your expenses. The expenses that are part of the amounts you can claim include:

- phone and internet expenses
- decline in value of equipment and furniture
- electricity and gas for heating, cooling and lighting.

A taxpayer can claim either the 80 cents per hour as a shortcut method, or the above expenses, if they chose. The ATO has published a series of occupation-specific fact sheets and information about employees working from home during and post Covid-19.

Self-education Expenses

Self-education expenses can be claimed, provided the study is directly related to either maintaining or improving current occupational skills or is likely to increase income from your current employment. If you obtain new qualifications in a different field through study, the expenses incurred are not tax deductible.

Typical self-education expenses include course fees, textbooks, stationery, student union fees and the depreciation of assets, such as computers, tablets and printers.

Higher Education Loan Program (HELP) repayments are not deductible. You must also reduce your claim by $250 of self-education expenses, which can include non-deductible amounts, such as childcare costs. This reduction is currently being reviewed and may be changed.

Motor Vehicle Deductions

If you use your motor vehicle for work-related travel, there are two choices on how you can claim. If the annual travel claim does not exceed 5000 kilometres, you can claim a deduction for your vehicle expenses on a cents-per-kilometre basis. This figure includes all your vehicle running expenses, including depreciation. The allowable rate for such claims changes annually. The rate for the 2021 and 2022 tax year is 72 cents per kilometre, and for 2019 and 2020 it was 68 cents per kilometre.

You do not need written evidence to show how many kilometres you have travelled, but you may be asked to show how you worked out your business kilometres. The ATO has flagged concerns that taxpayers are automatically claiming the 5000-kilometre limit regardless of the actual amount travelled. As mentioned earlier, you need to have incurred expenses in order to be able to claim a tax deduction.

If your business travel exceeds 5000 kilometres, you must use the logbook method to claim a deduction for your total car-running expenses based on the logbook business percentage over private use. Logbooks can be downloaded or purchased from all stationery stores.

To claim either of the above methods for your motor vehicle you need to show that you:

- travel on work-related journeys during the day/night. Say, to clients, various customers' premises, or to suppliers to pick up goods
- use your vehicle to drive to work-related conferences or meetings that aren't held at your usual place of work
- travel between two different places of employment – say job one to job two – and neither of these places of employment is at your home
- drive from a normal workplace to a different workplace, then back to where you would usually work (not home)
- drive from home to a workplace that isn't your usual place of work and then drive to your usual workplace – or directly home

- attend more than one workplace or site each day so you drive between them before driving home
- are required to carry bulky goods or heavy tools or equipment to and from work and you are not able to store them at work.

You cannot claim your motor vehicle costs if the trips are:

- related to travel from home to work or vice versa, even if you live a long way from your work
- reimbursed by your employer (you must have incurred and paid for the costs yourself).

Depreciation

Immediate deductions can be claimed for assets costing under $300 to the extent the asset is used to generate income. Such assets may include tools for tradespeople, calculators, briefcases, computer equipment and technical books purchased by an employee, or minor items of plant purchased by a landlord. Assets costing $300 or more used for income-producing purposes must be written off over their useful life. The amount of the deduction is generally determined by the asset's value, its effective life and the extent to which you use it for income-producing purposes.

Donations

Gifts or donations made to registered organisations are deductible. Ensure the receipt shows your donation is tax deductible. If you made donations to an approved organisation through workplace giving, you still need to record the total amount of your donations to claim them.

Your payment summary, or other written statement from your employer showing the donated amount, is sufficient evidence to support your claim. You do not need to have a receipt.

Also be aware that you need to pay the amount to get a deduction. Donations by family members or others on your behalf do not entitle you to claim a tax deduction. The payment must be paid by the person claiming the tax deduction.

Claim a Tax Deduction for Your Superannuation Contributions

Claiming a tax deduction for personal superannuation contributions is no longer restricted to the self-employed. The rules changed on 1 July 2017 to allow anyone under the age of 75 to be able to claim contributions made from their after-tax income to a complying superannuation fund as fully tax-deductible in the 2022 tax year. Any contributions you claim a deduction on will count towards your concessional contribution cap (mentioned next). Such a deduction cannot increase or create a tax loss to be carried forward (and hence is wasted from a tax deduction point of view).

If you're aged 67 or over, you will have to satisfy the work test to contribute, and if you're under 18 on 30 June, you can only claim the deduction if you earned income as an employee or business owner. Other eligibility criteria apply.

To claim the deduction, you will first need to lodge a notice of intent to claim or vary a deduction for personal contributions with your superannuation fund. This must be done before you lodge your tax return or before the end of the following income year.

Superannuation Contribution Limits

Ensure you maximise your superannuation contribution limits before the end of the financial year. The concessional (tax-deductible) contribution cap for the 2020 and 2021 tax year is $25,000, increasing to $27,500 from 1 July 2021 for the 2022 tax year. Concessional contributions include any contributions made by your employer, salary-sacrificed amounts and personal contributions claimed as a tax deduction by self-employed or substantially self-employed persons.

If you're making extra contributions to your super and breach the concessional cap, the excess contributions over the cap will be taxed at your marginal tax rate, although you can have the excess contribution refunded from your super fund. If you do not contribute up to these caps, you can carry forward the unused cap for up to five years and use this in later years to offset any excess contributions.

Similarly, the annual non-concessional (post-tax) contributions cap is $100,000 for the 2021 year, increasing to $110,000 from 1 July 2021. There is a three-year bring forward provision to allow three years of non-concessional contributions. In other words, the next three years can be brought forward to the current year. From 1 July 2021, individuals with a balance of $1.7 million or more are not eligible to make non-concessional contributions.

If your combined income is above $250,000, the contributions tax on concessional contributions is doubled, increasing from the normal 15 per cent rate to 30 per cent. This is called division 293 tax. It is a trap that many taxpayers get caught with. They receive an assessment for this tax, which is payable by the taxpayer, not the super fund, and wonder what it is.

Superannuation Co-contribution – Government Top-up

If you earn less than $56,112 in the 2020–2021 tax year and you make after-tax contributions to your superannuation, you may qualify for the superannuation co-contribution. The government will match after-tax contributions 50 cents for each dollar contributed up to a maximum of $500 for a person earning up to $41,112. The maximum then gradually reduces for every dollar of total income over $41,112, reducing to nil at $56,112. This is worth considering every year, as it will build up over time.

For 2021 the government paid out $122 million in superannuation co-contributions to 391,812 superannuation members (Commissioner of Taxation Annual Report 2020–21, p 211).

Consolidate your Super

For most employees, it makes a lot of sense to have your entire super in one place. You'll reduce the amount of fees you're paying, only receive one lot of paperwork and only have to keep track of one fund.

Consider consolidating the super funds you do have into one fund. Compare your funds to work out which best suits your needs. Important things to look at are fees and charges, the investment options available and life insurance cover. In particular, if you have insurance cover in a fund, check whether you can transfer or replace it in the new fund so you don't end up losing the benefit altogether. You can look at past investment performance as well, but remember it is no guarantee of how the fund will perform in the future.

Once you've chosen the fund you want to keep, contact them. They can help transfer the money from your other super funds.

From November 2019, the ATO has been proactively consolidating these unclaimed super monies into eligible active super accounts if an individual hasn't requested a direct payment or for it to be rolled over to a fund of their choice. You will be notified by the ATO if this has been done.

If you've moved around or changed jobs occasionally, your old super fund may have lost track of you, and you may miss out on some of your super when you need it. To find your lost super, check out SuperSeeker on the ATO website.

Consider Salary Sacrifice Arrangements

You may wish to review your remuneration arrangements with your employer. You can forego future gross salary in return for receiving exempt or concessionally taxed fringe benefits. You can also make additional superannuation contributions under a valid salary sacrifice arrangement.

Tax Residency and Covid-19

The tests used to ascertain your residency status for tax purposes are not the same as residency tests used for other purposes, such as immigration. The ATO publishes information on residency and the relevant tests. For non-residents temporarily in Australia as a result of Covid-19, the ATO has advised that if the client is in Australia temporarily for some weeks or months, then they will not become an Australian resident for tax purposes as long as they usually live overseas permanently and intend to return there as soon as they are able. The same applies to Australian residents that get caught overseas. If they are required to pay foreign income tax, that tax will be credited against their Australian tax bill. A person who is a tax resident pays less tax than a non-resident. Residents of Australia are taxed on their worldwide income with offsets for foreign taxes paid.

First Home Super Saver Scheme

The First Home Super Saver (FHSS) scheme allows you to save money faster for your first home with the concessional tax treatment of super. You can make additional voluntary salary-sacrificed superannuation contributions up to $15,000 per year (and $30,000 in total) into your complying superannuation fund, which can be withdrawn to help finance a first home deposit.

Compulsory superannuation employer contributions and contributions in respect of defined benefit funds are not eligible for the FHSS scheme. Various other eligibility conditions must be satisfied.

The FHSS scheme is primarily aimed at low- to middle-income earners.

Maximise Tax Offsets

Tax offsets directly reduce your tax payable and can add up to a sizeable amount. Eligibility for tax offsets generally depends on your income, family circumstances and conditions for particular offsets.

Taxpayers should check their eligibility for tax offsets, which include the low- and middle-income tax offset, senior Australians and pensioners offset and the offset for superannuation contributions on behalf of a low-income spouse.

From 1 July 2019, the tax offset for net medical expenses for disability aids, attendant care or aged care is no longer available.

Tax Agents: Beware Big Promises and Very Low Fees

As a tax agent for over 40 years, I have seen some notable frauds involving tax agents. Just because a person holds a position of trust, it does not mean that it will not be abused by unscrupulous people. Tax agents have been found guilty of selling tax file numbers and tax fraud on client refunds. We heard of a tax agent on Sydney's Northern Beaches who collected the employee tax deducted and kept it. He made some excuse about controlling funds and paying it to the ATO. But he didn't pay it on.

Like most things in life, you tend to get what you pay for. Tax preparation is no different. You should be careful about who you ask to prepare your return, so your tax affairs are reported correctly and you are able to prove your claims if the ATO ask any questions. Also be diligent and take personal responsibility for your affairs, lodgements and debt. If your refund is too good to be true, then you – or your agent – have probably broken the law.

Firstly, check your tax agent is registered with the Tax Agent Practitioners Board. All tax agents must be registered with this body and have a unique tax agent number. It's also recommended they're a member of a professional accounting organisation, such as Chartered Accountants Australia New Zealand (CAANZ), CPA

Australia or the Institute of Affiliate Accountants, so you know they're abiding by their licensing body's ethical standards.

Tax agents are not BAS agents. While tax agents can lodge income tax returns and BASs, BAS agents are not legally able to lodge income tax returns on behalf of their clients, nor are BAS agents able to charge for lodging income tax returns.

Tax agents use a specialised ATO Tax Agent Portal. They will never ask you for your myGovID credentials or seek to lodge your tax return through myTax. We have seen bookkeepers with good intentions do just that for their clients. It leaves them open to being prosecuted by the tax agents board, which does happen every year.

Every tax agent is legally obliged to take reasonable care. This means checking your tax history, ensuring you have documentation, such as receipts, and asking questions about your income, expenses and assets. They do not audit your records, but simply ask questions to ensure what they are provided is correct and in accordance with the law. They exercise a duty of care. In the past tax agents did not need to satisfy themselves about deductions, but could rely on what they were told; however, that has since changed. Also, they should only include information the client has provided to them (and not make it up).

Be aware of agents who:

- offer a very low fixed fee
- promise large refunds
- charge a percentage of your refund as a fee
- spend very little time with you or on your tax return
- don't ask for receipts
- don't ask questions or make claims that you can't substantiate
- ask you to sign blank or incomplete returns, or blank voluntary disclosure forms
- ask to lodge your tax return through the myTax website
- don't let you see, check and sign your tax return before it is lodged.

Make sure you check the tax return in detail before signing. All of your assessable income should have been reported and your deductions correctly recorded. After all, accountants are human and can make honest mistakes. Make sure you can back up every dollar of the claims.

Remember, ultimately, what gets lodged is your responsibility, and you are the one who has to pay the extra tax plus penalties and interest if anything is wrong on your tax return. In 2020, an unscrupulous tax agent (not us, of course) lodged tax returns for clients that had visited that accounting practice in previous years. They had all of their private information. They then proceeded to lodge the current year's tax returns, generating large tax refunds. They kept the refunds. It was only when those clients tried to lodge that year's tax return that the fraud was discovered.

Be Careful of Scams and Protect Your Identity

There has been a significant increase in Australians being targeted with scams related to Covid-19, fraud attempts and deceptive email and SMS schemes. If you're unsure whether an ATO interaction is genuine, do not reply. If you receive an SMS or email claiming to be from the ATO, check with the ATO first to confirm it is genuine or check with your tax agent. Do not make any emergency transfers to pay a tax debt if it has not been verified (especially with iTunes vouchers or Western Union). We had a client who operated a restaurant and was paying off a tax debt. When a purported tax officer rang him about his debt, he did not suspect it was a fraud. He was told to go to the bank and make an electronic transfer that day. He did and transferred some $2500. They rang him a little later and said they made a mistake and needed him to transfer another $1500. He became suspicious and rang us. We checked and it was indeed a fraudulent transaction. His tax account was in order, and he was up to date. Because the transaction happened in the same day, he was able to go back to the bank and get the first payment reversed. Had he left it overnight, he would have lost the money.

During this time of heightened scam activity, the ATO encourages individuals to:

- run the latest software updates to ensure operating system security is current
- update antivirus software
- always exercise caution when clicking on links and providing personal identifying information
- never share personal information on social media, such as your TFN, myGov or bank account details
- do not click on hyperlinks in an email or SMS – only via an independent search
- always access the ATO's online services directly via ato.gov.au or my.gov.au or the ATO app
- call the ATO on an independently sourced number to verify an interaction if in doubt
- don't click on a link, open an attachment or download a file if in doubt.

Scammers only need some basic details, such as your name, date of birth, address, myGov details or tax file number (TFN), to commit identity crime. We had a client whose identity was stolen. It took him two years to get it back. It may be difficult for you to get a job, a loan, rent a house or apply for government services or benefits. Ensure your digital identity, such as your myGovID, is secure. Your digital identity is unique to you and should never be shared. This enables others to access your personal data across multiple services, such as tax and health.

If you suspect your TFN or ABN has been stolen, misused or compromised, phone the ATO as soon as possible. The number is 1800 467 033, and you can call between 8.00 am and 6.00 pm

Monday to Friday so they can investigate and place additional protective measures on your account.

2022–23 Federal Budget

The 2022–23 Federal Budget was released on 29 March 2022 with effects flowing through into the 2022–23 tax year. While there is no certainty that the legislation will follow in the same way as the budget papers or press releases indicate, here is a summary of the tax effects of these measures and how you can access them:

- **Low- or middle-income living tax offset (LMITO).** This has been increased from $1080 to $1500 for the 2022 and 2023 tax years. It is not a tax handout, but instead an offset against tax payable. If no tax is payable, you do not receive the offset. From a tax-planning point of view, to obtain this offset, push your income up (through trust distributions dividend etc) to between $48,001 and $90,000. Below $37,000 the offset was increased to $675 (previously $255). It then scales up, with the full rebate applying when your income reaches $48,001 but is less than $90,001. It then scales back to nil, when your income reaches $126,001. Play the tax game to make sure you qualify for this (if possible).
- A one-off tax-exempt or tax-free payment of $250 as a 'cost of living' payment will be paid to a list of recipients of certain pensions and benefits.
- A tax deduction will be allowed for Covid-19 test expenses.

Accountants love working with excel spreadsheets to calculate the lowest tax payable based on different scenarios. The above changes make this extremely important. Do not underestimate how playing the tax rate game can materially reduce your tax payable.

21

Tax Tip 9: Year-end Tax Planning Tips for Investors

Many Australians invest in property, financial markets and other assets, both here and overseas. Over 5 million individuals receive dividend income each year ($93 billion in 2019), while 2.1 million report rental income totalling $44 billion. Capital gains of $20 billion was reported by almost 700,000 individuals, while more than 900,000 reported capital losses of $27 billion. Assessable foreign source income of almost $6 billion was reported by 730,000 individuals.

The ATO's data matching and information exchange capabilities continue to evolve and now cover many capital transactions and investment revenue streams both in Australia and overseas. It is therefore more important than ever to report investment income, including any income from overseas, and maintain accurate records. You must correctly calculate capital gains or losses on disposal and ensure you comply with the various rules and concessions available to investors.

Investment Income Deductions

You can claim a deduction for expenses incurred in earning interest, dividends or other investment income, but not if you receive an exempt dividend or other exempt income.

Examples of deductions include:

- account-keeping fees for an account held for investment purposes
- interest charged on money borrowed to buy shares and other related investments from which you derive assessable interest or dividend income
- ongoing management fees or retainers and amounts paid for advice relating to changes in the mix of investment
- a portion of other costs incurred in managing your investments, such as some travel expenses, investment journals, subscriptions and borrowing costs.

If you attend an investment seminar, you are only entitled to claim a deduction for the portion of travel expenses relating to some investment income activities.

Rental Properties

The ATO continues its focus on checking rental deductions and matching reported income against details from AirBnb and other providers. From the 2021 tax year, a multi-property rental schedule for individuals is required to be lodged with tax returns.

Covid-19 has raised several tax issues for rental property owners to consider, including:

- deductions for properties where tenants are not paying their full rent or have temporarily stopped paying rent as their income has been affected due to Covid-19
- reductions in rent for tenants whose income has been adversely affected by Covid-19 to enable these tenants to stay in the property

- assessable receipts of back payments of rent or an amount of insurance for lost rent
- interest deductions on deferred loan repayments for a period due to Covid-19
- cancellation of bookings due to Covid-19 for a property usually rented out for short-term accommodation, but that has also previously had some private use by the owner
- the private use of a rental property by the owner – for example, a holiday home to isolate in during Covid-19 – and adjusting the available tax deductions
- changes to advertising and other fees for short-term rental properties during Covid-19 due to no demand for the property.

Top 10 Tips – Common Mistakes Rental Owners Make

- **Apportioning expenses and income for co-owned properties.** If you own a rental property with someone else, you must declare rental income and claim expenses according to the legal ownership of the property. As joint tenants, your legal interest will be an equal split, and as tenants in common, you may have different ownership interests.
- **Making sure your property is genuinely available for rent.** Your property must be genuinely available for rent to claim a tax deduction. This means:
    - you must be able to show a clear intention to rent the property
    - advertising the property so that someone is likely to rent it and set the rent in line with similar properties in the area
    - avoiding unreasonable rental conditions

- an awareness that any related party discounts may limit your tax deduction; for example, if you rent your property at a discount to your parents or children.
- **Getting initial repairs and capital improvements right.** Repairs can only be claimed if they relate directly to wear and tear or other damage associated with the period the property was rented. For example, repairing the air-conditioning or part of a damaged floor can be deducted immediately. When you first purchase a property, all initial repairs to make the property fit for renting will not be immediately deductible. These form part of the cost base and are used to work out your capital gain or capital loss when you sell the property. Some costs may be depreciable. Be careful if you need to make major repairs such as a new roof, new bathroom, as these will be classified as an improvement and not immediately deductible. They will be building costs that you can claim at 2.5 per cent each year for 40 years from the date of completion.
- **Claiming borrowing expenses.** Special rules relate to borrowing expenses. If they are over $100, you can claim a deduction over five years in equal amounts. If the charge is $100 or less, the full amount is claimable. These include loan establishment fees, title search fees and costs of preparing and filing mortgage documents.
- **Claiming purchase costs.** Costs associated with the purchase of a property form part of the cost base of the property and cannot be claimed. These costs include conveyancing fees and stamp duty (for properties outside the ACT). Being part of the cost base, they reduce your capital gain when the property is sold.
- **Claiming interest on your loan.** Interest is claimed as a deduction on amounts borrowed to purchase a rental

property. It is the use to which the money is put that determines the deductibility. Hence if you use some of the money for a holiday, take a cruise, or a swimming pool at your home, that portion will not be deductible. Remember, it is not the security that determines the tax deductibility, it is what the money is used for.

- **Getting construction costs right.** Building costs, including extensions, alterations and structural improvements, can be claimed as capital works deductions. Under Division 43 of the *Income Tax Assessment Act 1936* you can claim a capital works deduction at 2.5 per cent of the construction cost for 40 years from the date the construction was completed. In cases where you have purchased a second-hand property and the previous owners have claimed capital works deductions, you will need to ask them to provide you with the details of what they have claimed so that you can claim the balance of any write-offs. If you can't obtain those details from the previous owner, you can use the services of a quantity surveyor to prepare what is called a QS report. This report will provide the details you need to claim the correct depreciation write-offs.

- **Claiming the right portion of your expenses.** Be careful if you rent your property to family or friends below market rate. You can't claim deductions when your family or friends stay free of charge or for periods of personal use. If you rent your property below market value, the deductions you claim will be limited. For example, if you rent a property to your parent at 50 per cent of the market rent, then only 50 per cent of all expenses will be claimable.

- **Ensure you keep records.** Make sure you keep all receipts to ensure you can prove any claims you make. Sometimes a property will be your sole and principal residence and then later become a rental property. When this happens, capital gains tax will apply when you sell that property. Ensure you keep records over the entire period you own a property. The ATO can review any claims, so ensure you keep your records for five years from the date you sell the property.

- **Make sure the capital gains/loss is calculated correctly.** There will be a time when you may wish to sell your rental property. This will create either a capital gain or a capital loss. Your cost base includes all costs associated with the purchase of the property (legal fees, stamp duty, etc) but must not include amounts already claimed as a deduction against rental income such as depreciation and capital works. A capital gain will be included in your tax return for the income year in which the contract is signed or becomes unconditional. If you make a capital loss, you can carry the loss forward and deduct it from capital gains in later years.

Owners of properties that are to be rented or are ready and available for rent can claim immediate deductions for a range of expenses, such as:

- interest on investment loans
- land tax
- council and water rates
- body corporate charges insurance
- repairs and maintenance
- agent's commission
- gardening
- pest control
- leases – preparation, registration and stamp duty
- advertising for tenants.

Landlords may be entitled to claim annual deductions for the declining value of depreciable assets, such as stoves, carpets and hot water systems. This includes capital works deductions spread over a number of years for structural improvements, like remodelling a bathroom.

Last year, changes were made that denied landlords the travel costs relating to inspecting, maintaining or collecting rent for a rental property.

Further to this, for properties acquired after 9 May 2017, deductions for the depreciation of plant and equipment for residential real estate properties are limited to outlays actually incurred on new items by investors. Hence they can no longer depreciate assets in the property at the time of purchase that are used. This does not apply to new properties or new assets.

Plant and equipment forming part of residential investment properties as of the 9 May 2017, will continue to give rise to deductions for depreciation until either the investor no longer owns the asset or the asset reaches the end of its effective life.

Make sure all income and expense claims are correctly apportioned between the owners of the rental property based on the ownership percentage.

Deductions for Vacant Land

Often from an investment point of view you may wish to hold vacant land to build a rental property or duplex in the future. Unfortunately, until it is income-earning the costs associated with holding this asset will not be deductible. If this is the case, we recommend you find a builder that needs a storage yard and rent it to them. That way it will become income-earning until you are ready to build and all holding costs will be deductible. Otherwise these costs will be capitalised and added to the cost base of the land. These holding costs include interest, rates, land tax, and so on. The government introduced changes to legislation to limit deductions claimed for holding vacant land, which received royal assent on 28 October 2019. These changes apply to costs incurred on or after 1 July 2019, even if the land was held before that date.

The exception to the above rules is if the land is held by a company or a super fund other than a self-managed superannuation fund. Frankly, I do not recommend you hold land in a company as you do not get the 50 per cent CGT discount in a company. For these entities, deductions for holding costs can continue to be claimed.

If you are carrying on a business such as farming, building (and need land to store heavy machinery or equipment) these expenses will be deductible.

Be clever with this one. If you hold vacant land and incur high interest costs, be proactive to ensure it is deductible. But remember, if it is deductible then it will not be added to the cost base of the land to reduce any future capital gain on its sale. This will be a tax-planning balancing act you need to be careful of. Also be aware that there may be GST implications if you subdivide and sell. If you hold vacant land, we suggest you check the ATO website. They have produced a great chart that assists to determine how they view these deductions. Then use the chart to ascertain the best method that works for you. Remember to be creative.

Residential Property and Non-residents

The ATO has continued to restrict deductions, increase tax and enact numerous measures to tax non-residents at a higher rate. If you are considering moving overseas, be very careful of this. Even your sole and principal residence at the time you move overseas will lose its tax-free status, which will be backdated to the date you acquired it – not the date you move overseas. The CGT main residence exemption will only be able to be claimed for disposals up until 30 June 2020. You needed to sell before 30 June 2020 or satisfy the 'life events test':

- you were a foreign resident (as defined by the *Income Tax Assessment Act 1936*) for a continuous period of years or less; and
- during that period, yourself, your spouse or child under 18 was diagnosed with a terminal medical condition, your spouse or child under 18 died, or the CGT event happened due to a marriage or relationship breakdown (a formal agreement must have been in place).

Remember, the disposal date is the date a contract was entered into, not the settlement date.

These rules also apply if a foreign resident dies. The estate will need to deal with the tax implications on the sale of any property held by the foreign resident, with the loss of all CGT concessions.

Be careful of this one. Be aware of the rules and consider them before making a decision to sell.

Cryptocurrencies and Crowdfunding

The ATO is now matching transaction data obtained from digital exchanges, so it is important to ensure cryptocurrency gains and losses are correctly reported. If you are currently, or have been, involved in acquiring or selling cryptocurrencies in the past, you need to be aware of the income tax consequences. These vary depending on the nature of your circumstances.

All cryptocurrency traders must keep appropriate records for income tax purposes. If you have dealt with a foreign exchange and/or cryptocurrency, there may also be taxation consequences for your transactions in the foreign country.

The tax consequences of crowdfunding vary depending on the nature of the arrangement, your client's role, promoter, intermediary or contributor and the circumstances.

With crypto and crowdfunding, the tax laws apply to the investment and financial activity in the usual manner that applies to any person carrying on a business (review Chapter 19 on share trading for an outline of this). For example, buying goods and services, shares, or lending money, is the same as investments and financial activity conducted under crowdfunding and crypto buying and selling.

If you are involved in cryptocurrencies or crowdfunding, you should ensure you obtain professional advice. The ATO has issued a tax ruling on the treatment of both. It has also confirmed that they are presently data matching all transactions from various exchanges. We have even seen audits as a result of this data matching.

Also be aware that, under tax law, you are taxed on any profits you make in a financial year. This means profits realised or unrealised (depending on your circumstances and the manner in which the tax rulings apply to you) in the year ended on 30 June. If you reinvest that profit into further investments, it does not always reduce your tax payable. A point I make very clear to clients is one of tax risk. For example, let's say that for the year ended 30 June 2021, you have made $2 million profit on Bitcoin and reinvested that back into, say, Ethereum coins. Let's also assume that on 1 July, those Ethereum coins drop in value to zero, so you have a real cash flow problem. Now, you have tax payable on $2 million but no way of paying that tax as the money has been lost in a subsequent tax year. We therefore recommend all investors cash out sufficient funds to meet their tax liabilities. After all, the ATO is yet to accept digital currency in payment of a tax bill.

Capital Gains Tax Planning

Careful planning should be undertaken in planning the timing of the disposal of appreciating assets, which may trigger a capital gain. It is important to recognise that CGT is triggered when you enter into a contract for the sale of a CGT asset rather than on its settlement.

This is particularly important where the contract date and settlement of the contract straddle year-end. In these circumstances, it may be preferable from a cash flow perspective to defer the sale of the CGT asset to the subsequent year. Other relief may be available, such as a capital loss sold on another asset.

Care should also be taken to ensure an eligible asset is retained for the 12-month holding period required under the CGT discount. Also, be aware the CGT discount is not available on any capital gain accrued after 8 May 2012 if you were a foreign resident or temporary resident at any time after that date.

As always, plan any event, consider the CGT consequences and the manner in which the Tax Act will interface with that transaction. You always have the option to defer signing a contract, enter into other contracts to offset any gains and generally manage the tax aspect. Do not allow yourself to be a victim on this through being tardy. Take your time, get advice and make sure there are no unintended consequences. In Chapter 19, I have covered some of these known as 'holding rules' and the 'wash test'. Go back and review if these rules will catch you out.

The ATO publishes guidance on capital gains tax. Refer also to the previous chapters in this book for more on this very complex area. Ensure you keep proper records for all investments for at least five years after a capital gains tax event occurred.

Foreign Investments

If you are an Australian resident with overseas assets, you need to include any capital gains or losses you make on those assets in your tax return. You also may have to include income you receive from overseas interests. You are required to declare all income earned, even if you haven't physically received it back in Australia. Australia has tax treaties with most countries. This means that you may be entitled to a credit for any tax paid in an overseas jurisdiction.

Also, don't think you can hide income earned overseas. As an Australian resident you are taxed on worldwide income. The ATO has information exchange agreements with revenue authorities in many foreign jurisdictions.

22

Tax Tip 10: Year-end Tax Planning Tips for Small Businesses

Tax Tips for Small Businesses

The financial year ends on 30 June each year. A business is taxed on the profit earned in that 12-month period. Financial statements are prepared that reflect the trading for the year, plus a statement of financial position (balance sheet) as of 30 June. Hence, this one day of the year becomes etched in stone as the financial position of the company. It will also be used for comparison purposes. It is therefore important that this is recognised and managed. It is too late to consider any insolvency or poor financial position after this date.

Every business owner should:

- monitor their current trading position to ensure the profits meet whatever criteria they are aiming for. In some cases, banks or other licensing authorities may have loan covenants or financial ratios that must meet certain rules.
- ensure the statement of financial position (balance sheet) of the company as of 30 June meets any banking or regulatory requirements, such as in the building industry or with any bank loans or banking covenants.

It may sound strange but this one day of the year is the day when all financial statements are prepared and become the measure of the business for many years to come.

Some of the above cannot be fixed after 30 June, but a company may be able to do certain things before 30 June, like increase share capital, seek additional funds, work to complete any partly completed work to invoice it, sell any redundant stock, just to name a few. Plus, of course, you should do any tax planning that may lessen any tax payable on the profits earned in that financial year.

This pre-30 June period is a valuable time that needs to be spent with your professional advisor to not only review the year that has passed but to also consider what tips are there to help you in the future. To facilitate this, a business needs to ensure its bookkeeping is up to date. If there are any complex tax issues, this is the time to seek outside professional help. This help may include refinanced debt, losses, restructures, capital gains tax, personal services income, trust declarations and distributions, and private company loans.

Listed below are areas that need to be considered in your year-end tax planning. Review them carefully and review how they relate to your business. As always, not all of them will apply to your particular situation. While I am sure, as a business owner, you will know most of the below, it always pays to remind yourself of items you may have missed or forgotten.

Covid-19 – New Rules to Consider

The Use of Past Year Tax Losses

Due to the government being overzealous with assistance to small business, a loss carry-back rule was introduced. Effectively this allows a company that paid tax in 2019 and then had a loss in the 2020 or 2021 tax year to carry back that loss and get a refund of the tax paid for 2019. Watch this one, as we have seen people close their doors because of Covid-19 and lose the ability to claw back this previous tax paid. Now, under the legislation, losses can be carried back or carried forward to future income years. For example, a tax loss in the 2021 tax year can be carried forward indefinitely provided the business continues to satisfy the tax loss tests listed below. These tests must be satisfied before 'carried forward tax losses' can be offset against profits.

For example, if because of Covid-19 or any other reason your business were to cease trading (or even change to a totally different business) and there were to be a major change in shareholding, the ability to claim prior year losses would be lost. There are two rules that need to be met to enable carried forward tax losses to be used: a continuity of ownership test and a same or similar business test. A change in ownership or a restructure can mean the loss of the ability to use carried forward tax losses. Be careful of this one, as sometimes when you seek a new investor to help you through a difficult time, there may be some unintended consequences.

Bad Debts

If you have an amount owing on your books from a client and there is no possibility of recovery, it would pay to write it off in the books before 30 June. If, by some miracle, you recover the debt, you can always record it as income in the year it is received. If you prepare your tax return on a cash basis, writing off bad debts will have no effect. This only applies to accrual accounting. All businesses should review all outstanding debtors in April/May to assess their likely recoverability. Remember also to claim back any GST, if applicable, to any bad debts written off.

Trading Stock

Trading stock or closing stock is a credit on your profit and loss statement. Hence the higher the stock value the higher the net profit (and tax) will be. To some this sounds confusing. Hence by taking up a lower value you reduce the taxable profit. Closing stock in one year becomes opening stock in the following year. It can be used as a tax deferral method. Under the *Income Tax Assessment Act 1936*, stock can be valued at the lower of cost, market value or net realisable value. If, because of Covid-19, you are able to show a lower value for trading stock and this will reduce your taxable income, you should do so. If, however, you are recording a loss for another reason (like reduced trading, asset write-offs, etc) you may want to value your closing in stock at a higher figure and hence move some of the loss to a future tax year.

Trading stock is a tool that can be used effectively to move profits from one year to the next, all in accordance with the tax act. For example, you may need to show a profit that can be offset against foreign tax credits, foreign withholding tax or even company franking credits. Some of these will be lost (or, in the case of franking credits, converted to tax losses). I had a client who would have lost $60,000 in foreign withholding tax if we hadn't used this system to claw it back.

To ease the burden of actually doing a stocktake, businesses can use the simpler trading stock rules if their trading stock does not vary by more than $5000 per year.

Amounts Received as JobKeeper Payments

Businesses that received JobKeeper payments need to include these as income. They are taxable receipts. Of course the business will be able to claim all payments made to employees as wages or superannuation. To receive JobKeeper payments, a business must have paid its employees at least $1500 per fortnight. Hence the amount received will effectively offset this cost.

Where you are making these claims, ensure you maintain your documentation in case the ATO seeks to review your entitlement. You were required to obtain a declaration from all employees before you made the claim. Keep these declarations on file. I expect that in 2022, the ATO may start asking for copies of these declarations

I had a business come to me for help, due to an ATO audit. They had claimed JobKeeper payments for five different companies, none of which actually employed any staff. The ATO is aware of behaviours and methods taxpayers have used which include falsifying records or revising activity statements to meet the fall in turnover test or failing to pass on the full $1500 (per fortnight) JobKeeper payment to eligible employees. The ATO has indicated it will focus on the application of the decline in turnover test, for example, where actual and projected turnover have significantly diverged, as well as issues identified in PCG 2020/4 Schemes in relation to the JobKeeper payment. To date, other than flagrant abuse (by the business noted above, which did not end up as a client), I haven't seen any activity in this area as yet. In respect of my firm's clients, we have all the back-up material should the ATO request it, so that none of our clients will have any issues with any audit of JobKeeper payments.

(As an aside, the business that came to us for help had also attempted to claim high GST refunds to which they were not entitled to. They would not make a full admission of their wrongdoing, hence we could not act for them. It is my personal view that they will eventually receive a custodial sentence when the audit is completed.)

Cash Flow Boost

Again, the government was really trying to help businesses through a difficult time. If your business qualified, the amounts received as the 'cash flow boost' were tax-free payments. The amounts were paid from March 2020 to September 2020. These payments were not subject to GST.

The issue going forward will be, because the cash flow boost is exempt income, if and when it is distributed to trust beneficiates or shareholders as unfranked dividend, whether those recipients may be taxed on it. The government intended the cash flow boost to be used to support the business and hence expected that no such distributions would occur. However, in real life this may not be the case. With trusts, provided the trust deed allows streaming of various types of income, it may be possible to flow the above out to beneficiaries if its tax-free status can be streamed. With companies, unfortunately, the payment can only be an unfranked dividend.

Zombie Businesses – Those in Dire Financial Distress

It is a fact that Covid-19 has caused many businesses cash flow difficulties or severe financial distress to reconsider their viability or close. The provision of government support payments, such as cash flow boost, JobKeeper, rent relief, various state and territory grants and temporary changes to the insolvency rules, might have helped some to survive for a short period. However, as all of these support measures are at an end, many of these businesses may need to reconsider their options. The press calls these businesses 'zombie businesses', meaning they are dead businesses that are still operating. When do they decide to throw in the towel? The answer is never easy.

Under the Corporations Law, a company is deemed insolvent when it cannot pay its debts as and when they fall due. Under the law it should cease trading when the directors determine that to be the case. Indicators of insolvency are: continuing trading losses, cash flow difficulties, and difficulties selling stock or collecting debts. When a company trades after its directors determine it is insolvent, those directors can be held personally liable for all debts incurred after the point of insolvency. Also, directors can be personally liable for amounts owing to the ATO for GST, Superannuation and PAYG instalments.

This is a complex area that has both income tax and corporations law implications. We have, on many occasions, assisted directors or business owners who are facing serious financial hardship with their application for release from their tax debts. The ATO's approach and rules are set out in PS LA 2011/17 Debt relief, waiver and non-pursuit. Be careful with the non-pursuit provisions, as the ATO has a habit of restoring these debts at a later time, especially if a refund occurs many years later.

Be aware that it is sometimes prudent and the correct course of action to cease trading if a business is insolvent. The directors have obligations under the Corporations Act. They also should not be continuing if it is a lost cause. There are rules, but nothing stops a business owner from commencing a new business when the former business is required to cease trading. This is known (by the ATO) as legal or illegal phoenixing, depending on how it is actioned. A 'phoenix' is described in Greek Mythology as a long-lived bird that obtains new life by rising from the ashes of its predecessor. If you need to start again, make sure you follow the ATO rules and even discuss the matter with an insolvency expert. If you make this transition correctly there will be no repercussions. We have assisted with thousands of these over my 40 years in practice.

Good Record Keeping and Honesty

In Chapter 12, 'Why You Must Do Things Legally – The Penalties' I covered the implications of trying to minimise your tax by defrauding the ATO. This can take many forms, ranging from poor to no record keeping, to outright dishonesty. In today's era of data matching, you cannot afford to get it wrong. Proper record keeping, keeping receipts to substantiate your claims and proper recording of all entries are essential, which includes declaring all cash transactions.

Some of this will include:

- recording cash income and expenses
- accounting for personal drawings

- recording goods for your own use
- keeping private expenses separate from business expenses
- keeping valid tax invoices for creditable acquisitions when registered for GST
- keeping adequate stock records
- keeping adequate records to substantiate motor vehicle claims.

This will be the only way you will be able to sleep at night. Use the system, but do so legally.

In 2021, the ATO continued its audit activity on high net worth individuals. We have already worked on a few of these. They started with the top 500 high net worth taxpayers, then moved to the next 5000. They are currently working on the next 5000 category. We expect this will eventually filter down to all businesses, similar to the USA where they conduct reviews. The main purpose of the audit (in the first instance) is to look at record keeping. They want to assure themselves that the business being reviewed has adequate and proper accounting systems to identify its income correctly.

The ATO is in its 17th year of data matching. This enables them to align income from many sources to your tax account. When you lodge your income tax return, if any discrepancies arise, they are quick to highlight these and send a 'please explain' letter. The ATO has increased resources to tackle all areas and in fact usually yields a profit on their time spent doing so. They also have at their disposal industry benchmarks that help detect any variations in business patterns like gross profit percentages. This will help them detect any undeclared income.

My point is, don't under-declare your income or try to hide transactions. The ATO will find out and fine you accordingly. In Australia, we have a self-assessment system, which means the onus is on you, the taxpayer, to correctly report your income.

Depreciation Claims

All businesses can claim a write-off of deprecation on assets purchased and used in their business. Usually such assets are depreciated over their useful life or according to a formula. Asset write-offs are covered in more detail in Chapter 18, 'Tax Tips 6 – Asset Write-offs'. The government, in an effort to stimulate the economy during Covid-19, introduced new instant asset write-off rules up to a value of $150,000. While this is covered in an earlier chapter, it is useful to review some of this from a different angle.

As always with asset write-offs or depreciation, the amount that can be written off will depend on the date the asset is first used or installed ready for use for a taxable purpose. Where a business is registered for GST, the threshold is calculated on a GST-exclusive basis. If a business is not registered for GST, the threshold is calculated on a GST-inclusive basis.

In respect of motor vehicles used in your business, the instant asset write-off is limited to the business portion of the depreciation car limit of $60,733 for the 2022 income tax year. You cannot claim the excess cost of the car under any other depreciation rules.

If the cost of the asset is not available for the instant asset write-off deduction, it can be allocated to the general small business pool and depreciated at 15 per cent for the first year and 30 per cent each year thereafter. If you sell the asset, then a balancing adjustment is needed whereby the sale price is credited to the pool. This has the effect of reducing future depreciation claims on the balance of the small business pool.

Company Tax Rates and Imputation Credits

Most small businesses will have an aggregated turnover of less than $50 million. In this case they will pay tax at 25 per cent for the 2022 income tax year (26 per cent for the 2021 year). If a company receives more than 80 per cent of its income as passive income the tax rate will be 30 per cent.

This is covered in Chapter 6, 'Tax Rates for Different Entities'.

In order to qualify for the lower company tax rate:

- A company (or group) must have an aggregated turnover of less than $50 million. This includes the turnover of the company and all affiliated or group entities.
- No more than 80 per cent of the company's assessable income can be base rate entity passive income.

If a company does not qualify, then the full company tax rate of 30 per cent applies.

Small Business Income Tax Offset

A small business entity will be eligible for a small business tax offset of up to $1000 for the 2021 and 2022 income years. To qualify, a business must operate as a sole trader business or receive income from a partnership that is shown as 'small business income' (not rents or passive income). The aggregated turnover for the 2022 year must be less than $5 million. The offset rate is 13 per cent for the 2021 tax year and 16 per cent for the 2022 tax year and is an offset to the income tax payable on the portion of an individual's taxable income that is their 'total net small business income'.

The ATO will work out the offset based on the net small business income earned as a sole trader and share of net small business income from a partnership or trust, as reported in the income tax return.

Private Company Loans to Directors and Shareholders

We often see small businesses where the directors have simply borrowed money from their company and not shown these withdrawals as either wages or loans. A company is a separate legal entity to yourself. The company bank account is not your personal bank account. The two should be kept separate. Under tax law, amounts withdrawn from a business are either wages, loans in accordance with a documented loan agreement or unfranked dividends. If the first two items cannot be proven, the default position (with dire tax consequences) applies. We had a new client who withdrew money from the sale of part of their business. The ATO audited them shortly after the sale. In the absence of the above determinations, the amounts drawn were treated as deemed unfranked dividends. The tax concerned was in excess of $2 million. It pays to decide in advance how to treat these withdrawals and document them accordingly.

Generally, to avoid any of the above, it is best to enter into what is referred to as a 'Division 7A loan agreement'. All accountants have an ATO approved format for these. They require a minimum interest and principal repayments over a specified loan term – seven years if the loan is unsecured or 25 years if the loan is secured.

Tax Write-offs at 120 per cent of Expenditure and Inflation Uplift

In the 2022–23 Federal Budget, the government announced the following assistance to businesses. When these changes are legislated and the criteria is clear, ensure you take advantage of these (if possible).

For businesses and employers, a 120 per cent tax deduction will be available:

- For expenses and depreciating assets that support digital adoption, such as portable payment devices, cyber security systems and subscriptions to cloud-based services (limited to $100,000 in each qualifying year).
- For expenses incurred on external training courses provided to employees.

In both of the above, for the 2022 year, the extra 20 per cent tax deduction is claimable in the 2023 tax year, even though the expenditure was incurred in the 2022 tax year.

The budget has also announced changes to the GST and PAYG instalment uplift amounts. Instead of calculating this uplift at 10 per cent the government is reducing it to 2 per cent.

23

Tax Tip 11: Year-end Tax Planning Tips for Trusts

Why Use a Trust?

Within a business structure, it is common to use a mixture of trusts and companies. Each have their place. It was reported that the late Alan Bond (former chairman of Bond Corporation) had 248 trusts. I remember reading the article about him in the BRW Rich List. While this could be said to be an accountant's dream from a fee point of view, it is obvious that there must have been a benefit. Trusts, similar to companies, allow assets to be held in them separately to the persons owning the entity. There are three important reasons why you may wish to hold an asset in a company or trust structure. These are:

1. Asset protection – to shelter your assets from creditors or any trading entity that may experience financial difficulties.
2. To allow ownership movements such as investors to own a varying piece of the pie.
3. For tax reasons – which I will cover in more detail later.

In the case of Alan Bond, he went bankrupt and served time in prison, yet his family to this day is still counted as one of the richest in Australia. He made massive profits from share trading in Bond Corporation, all of which were earned in his various trusts. None were attributed to him personally and were able to become claimed by his creditors when he went bankrupt.

As noted above, if you want to sell part of a business or property this is easier if you simply sell part of the company that owns it, or you sell additional units in a unit trust. It means the asset ownership stays in the entity and only the underlying owners will vary.

Think of a trust as a vehicle that allows flexibility. A trust can operate a business, be a passive holder of assets or do anything a natural person or company can do. With a trust, the owners can be employees and draw a wage or alternatively receive a distribution of the net income of the trust. As a tax planning tool, there is no entity that is better in certain situations. But be aware that a trust is not always the best structure.

Here are 10 things (both positive and negative) to consider when deciding what structure to use:

1. A company does not get the 50 per cent CGT discount. Hence if you hold assets, you are well advised to use a trust structure.

2. Companies pay tax on every dollar earned at the company tax rate (25–30 per cent). Individuals have a tax-free threshold of $20,800.

3. You cannot pay a wage to a person (or you are not supposed to) who does not work in the business from a tax point of view. Hence, non-working spouses should not be paid a salary up to the tax threshold. This does not apply to trusts, which can distribute to anyone.

4. If you are a member of a church or religious group and wish to donate a portion of your income to that group,

you can make them a beneficiary of your trust and pay that distribution before 30 June in a before-tax manner. You cannot do this with a company.

5. A trust, providing it distributes its income, does not pay tax. Hence all profits are distributed before tax. It becomes the problem of the beneficiaries to pay tax on income distributed to them.

6. With trusts you can play the tax game. Accountants love working their spreadsheet magic to calculate the most tax effective manner to distribute profits.

7. Subject to family tax elections and anti-avoidance measures, a trust can distribute to other trusts within the family group. This is especially important if a trust in the group has carried forward tax losses. The head trust can cascade its income to the trust with the carried forward tax losses.

8. Just a point on the above, a trust can only distribute profits. Any losses are trapped in the trust and cannot be distributed. Hence if you consider the trust you are creating will have losses in the early years, it would pay to re-think the structure being used.

9. You may wish to keep certain assets in a trust for asset protection reasons. The trust can then charge a licence fee or rent to a trading company for the use of those assets. This helps keep the assets away from creditors if the company were to go into liquidation.

10. In your group structure you need a mixture of companies for general trading and to assist with limiting your personal liability and trusts as a means to play the tax rate game.

So what do I recommend? Frankly there is a no 'one shoe fits all' situation. With a small trading business, a company is often the best structure. The entity will generally not own assets and simply be representing to the world what it does. If there are a number of owners, or as the business grows, you may consider using the company as a corporate trustee and dropping a trading trust under the company. There are some roll-over relief measures to allow this. The means the company is only trading in its capacity as trustee of the trust. Profits will then be paid to the beneficiaries of the trust. This is probably the second most common structure. After this, the web gets thicker. If the business is to own property, this would definitely be put into either a unit (property) trust or a family discretionary trust.

As mentioned earlier in this book, it is important to be ahead of your game when it comes to tax. If you are using a trust structure this is especially important as you need to know roughly what the year will look like, net income and tax wise, before 30 June.

Make Trust Distributions at the End of the Financial Year

It has always been the case that trustees of discretionary trusts are required to make and document resolutions on how trust income should be distributed to beneficiaries before the end of a financial year. Generally, this can simply be to pay Beneficiary A $10,000 and Beneficiary B $10,000, with the balance going to Beneficiary C. Of course, the correct names of each beneficiary must be shown.

The trustee of the trust needs to prove it has made this resolution before 30 June. In the past, most accountants prepared them after the financial accounts were prepared and inserted the net profit into the resolution. Unfortunately the ATO has ruled this is not acceptable. It has even audited these and looked into the date the document was created to prove the resolution was not made before 30 June. It is important to have evidence such as file notes, signed minutes, an exchange of correspondence to prove that they were prepared before June 30. It is not necessary to have accounts prepared before the resolution is determined.

If the ATO can prove a valid resolution has not been made, then either the default beneficiaries will be credited with the net income or the trustee will be assessed at the highest marginal tax rate on the basis that no beneficiary is presently entitled to the net income of the trust.

Streaming of Trust Capital Gains and Franked Dividends to Beneficiaries

When a trust makes various forms of income – such as capital gains, exempt income or dividends – it may be useful to allocate these to certain beneficiaries and hence retain their character. For example there may be franking credits associated with dividends. You may want to stream these to a beneficiary that will get a refund rather than to a beneficiary that is in a high tax bracket (say 47 per cent) and be forced to pay top-up tax on this extra income. The trust deed needs to allow this provision and the trust resolution needs to reflect this streaming.

The streaming rules are complex and were made even more complex by a high court case in 2010 referred to as the Bamford Case. The purpose of the above is simply to highlight that they apply. In all cases, you should seek professional help on this. Especially to ensure your trust deed has been amended to cater for the above.

Deemed Dividends of Unpaid Trust Distributions (UPEs)

This is a complicated area of trust law. It has always been common practice with a trust to have what is referred to in the industry as a 'bucket company'. The term comes from an entity receiving the overflow amounts from a trust. The best way to describe this is with an example. Say the net income of the trust is $200,000. You have three beneficiaries that you can give income to. The tax payable for income up to $18,200 is nil. The balance of $26,799 is taxed at 19 per cent or $5091.81. This times three is $15,275.43. There is still $65,000 to distribute. The next tax bracket is 32.5 per cent, moving up to 37 per cent then 45 per cent. Hence, to distribute this to the above three beneficiaries would result in 32 per cent or more tax being paid. The company tax rate for passive income is 30 per cent or 25 per cent for non-passive income. So it would make sense to distribute the balance to a company and for it to be taxed let say at the highest rate of 30 per cent – effectively $19,500. Of course, the above could be cut and diced may ways and the figures amended to give the best result.

Now it gets interesting. If the above distribution is paid to a company on the books but not physically paid as cash it will be treated as an unpaid distribution – an unpaid present entitlement (UPE). Any UPEs owed by a trust to a related private company beneficiary that arises on or after 1 July 2016 will be treated as a loan by the company if the trustee and the company are controlled by the same family group.

If you use a bucket company, it is important that the distribution be actually paid. To assist with this, the money could be paid and investments be held in the bucket company's name. If the distribution is not paid, the bucket company should enter into a complying Division 7A loan agreement and repayments made.

To prevent a deemed dividend being applied by the ATO in respect of unpaid distributions, a complying loan agreement must be entered into before the company's annual income tax return is lodged.

Stop Press

In February 2022, the government announced changes to trust laws that are currently under consultation. At the time of printing, it is not known the full extent of these changes nor how they will affect future decisions going forward. The changes are said to target how trusts distribute income to family groups. There is an integrity rule contained within section 100A of the tax act that the government is seeking to use, even though it lost a High Court case on this. The result may be to limit the members of a group that can receive distributions. A key measure will be that distributions are actually paid to the beneficiary and not to that person's parents for example. There are also circular arrangements that will be caught, however these were always marginal and generally not used by reputable accountants. Until the legislation is finalised it is not known what the full impact of these changes will be.

Part 4

How to Manage Your Business and Your Money Better

Unfortunately, it is true that education around managing money, simple tax matters and an outline of how money truly works is lacking. It may seem odd, but those who excel in creating massive wealth share this knowledge. However, the general population does not. There is also some incorrect information out there, generated by mistaken well-meaning people, but people who have never been in business or never created wealth (for themselves). The wealthy do help by passing on tips, but sometimes this is lost in the mainstream of being a worker and having the nine-to-five type of mentality that follows from it. Such business education is lacking in schools, which results in school leavers having no basic money, investment or tax knowledge. If they are lucky, they may have their parents as role models. If not, they will be sadly unprepared to enter the workforce, save for their own future retirement or have any basic understanding of the tax system. Given that many will in fact go into a small business for themselves means the problem becomes an issue for society.

In this section, I will cover some very basic information that forms the foundation of being financially successful. I will also give you some tools that you can use to create an abundance for yourself. Remember the airplane safety message: 'Fit your own oxygen mask first so you can help others.' Become wealthy so you can be a valuable member of society and help those less fortunate than you. Some of this information is extremely basic, so if you already know it, just skim over it. I never cease to be amazed at how little some business owners know about these areas. Yes, they are good at what they do, being a plumber, electrician, computer programmer and so on, but when it comes to business and tax skills, they have never been exposed to these at the level discussed in this book. For myself, it is something I have been doing for over 40 years every day. For a business owner, it is something they may do once a month or once a year.

The following chapters will help you apply the lessons listed earlier in the book, that you need to know, a kind of summary of the things that will ensure you do not fall into the same pitfalls of others. This details where you can go for help and the tools that are out there to help you.

I have assembled the following eight money tips to help readers with these basic points. Some are self-evident; some you may already know but have forgotten. They come from my many years as an accountant and business advisor to many thousands of people just like you. They also come from what I have learned from my own experience and from the successful (and the not-so-successful clients) that have either been my clients or clients of the accounting firms I have owned and operated for the past 40 years.

24

Money Tip 1: Know Your Business KPIs

KPIs are the key performance indicators on the health and drivers of your business. It is amazing how many businesses are run by their owners by the 'seat of their pants'. In other words, the owner has no idea of the true cost structure of the business; they guess everything. This can be made worse by accountants completing the financial statements and income tax returns nearly nine months after the end of the financial year. Bad luck if the business has been losing money; they have now lost another nine months of trading losses.

I often have a conversation around overheads, break-even points and how the business is going according to the owners. In most cases, these 'seat of the pants' views are simply wrong.

One case that comes to mind was a food wholesale company. They delivered smallgoods to shops, restaurants and other small establishments. The owner was at pains to show me why he was making a great profit. I asked him why, if they were making such great profit, was their tax behind? Why were they three months behind in their rent? His reply was that he just needed a little extra capital to buy more stock that he could sell and all of his problems would be over. Every time we tried to work out his true profit, there were so many timing errors, a lack of a proper stocktake that the true position was masked. Eventually, when I sat down and estimated the timing errors and the stock levels, the owner wouldn't face that he was trading below his break-even point.

He did not believe, or perhaps didn't want to face, that he wasn't covering his overheads.

The business closed owing over $2 million to creditors and nearly $1 million in loans from family members (who believed that he only needed a short-term fix). The family supported this person and believed what he was saying. Because of that, they lost their house and all their life savings. Needless to say, the tax office did not get the GST owing or the PAYG deducted from staff wages paid. The staff also missed out on having their superannuation paid.

All because the owner would not take stock of the true cost of running the business. He should have either increased his prices or closed his doors.

A business must be run with the owner's finger on the pulse, every day, to measure that a business is viable, profitable and meeting it obligations. All public companies do just that, with daily, weekly and monthly reporting.

For example, at one time, I was the company accountant for Kaiser Aluminium. We were in Bridge Street in Sydney. This company had its head office in Oakland, San Francisco, with operations all over the world. It was a requirement that by the seventh working day after month end, all subsidiaries telexed (indicates how long ago this was!) their results to Oakland, California. There were no excuses – they must be sent. The same was the case at Consolidated Press Holdings. All subsidiaries were required to send weekly reports into head office.

With direct bank feeds into various accounting software, there is no excuse for not knowing how you are tracking in your business.

Let me break down what the KPIs mean and how to decide what KPIs you should monitor.

KPIs fall into two broad categories:

- Profit and loss KPIs, such as sales, cost of sales, gross profit, overheads, break-even points and variable and fixed costs.
- Balance sheets or net position KPIs, such as stock on hand, debtors, creditors, cash at bank.

A business succeeds or fails based on its profit and loss. A business must either break-even or make a profit to survive. Of course, we all want to make a profit. Hence you must know your break-even point. This is the level of sales you need to cover your variable and fixed costs.

Let's look at this analytically and the picture will be clearer:

Figure 13 Example of a Profit and Loss Statement

	Example 1	Example 2	Example 3	Example 4
Sales	1,000,000	750,000	450,000	1,500,000
Direct costs				
Purchases – goods etc at 25%	250,000	187,500	112,500	375,000
Direct wages	68,000	68,000	68,000	68,000
Supplies	5600	5600	5600	5600
Total indirect costs	323,600	261,100	186,100	448,600
Gross Profit	676,400	488,900	263,900	1,051,400
Indirect costs				
Rent	15,000	15,000	15,000	15,000
Office and owners' wages	180,000	180,000	180,000	180,000
Other overheads	125,000	125,000	125,000	125,000
Total direct costs	320,000	320,000	320,000	320,000
Net Profit/(–Loss)	356,400	168,900	–56,100	731,400
Break-even point	473,093	490,898	545,661	456,534

Direct costs have some variable and fixed elements. Variable costs are items associated with your products. In the above example, we have assumed the cost of what is sold averages 25 per cent. Hence, there is a 75 per cent gross profit margin. But shop wages and some shop expenses will be fixed up to what one or two salespeople can handle. You can't keep the business open with half a person, as required in example 3. Then other costs will be fixed. They are incurred even if you do not sell one item. From Figure 13, it becomes readily apparent that the business must sell around $450,000 in products just to cover costs. At $1 million sales, it makes a great profit. At $450,000 in sales, it is losing $56,100. It can't go on losing that amount. But many businesses do. They think that they are making 75 per cent on every sale, that on $450,000 they should have $337,500 to cover their costs, but overheads and other costs swallow up that gross profit margin with the net result being a loss. Without doing a proper set of accounts the true position is hidden. Even in the previous example, you can see that the break-even point moves, and that net profit is not that easy to know unless you do a true reconciliation of all costs. This is why having a real-time profit and loss computation is so vital.

When we talk to clients, we calculate a rough break-even point that includes what the owners want to make as a salary. Let's assume that number is $25,000 per week. We request at the end of every week the owner look at their sales and whether they have achieved that break-even figure. It is amazing how, say, by Thursday, when the target looks like it will be missed, clients can magically find more sales, maybe ring that extra client to see if they need more. Be proactive to bring to the business more sales to make the weekly target. When the target becomes too easy, we then lift it a little. We keep doing this to keep the business pushing to new levels. But at all times we keep monitoring the costs. We do not want the overheads to blow out above the new sales levels, which sometimes can happen.

There are many other KPIs a business can track, as previously noted. What you track will depend on the type of business being operated. However, using online accounting systems such as Xero, QuickBooks or MYOB with input directly from your bank (bank feeds) will ensure you know your real-time position. Any business, no matter how small, should use the above to keep constant control of where their business is heading. After all, what you cannot track, you cannot control.

25

Money Tip 2: Make a Profit

Success depends upon previous
preparation, and without such preparation,
there is sure to be a failure.
Confucius

This chapter heading may seem a strange point to make, but can I say, I have seen so many situations where a business is not making a profit. Of course, losses can only be sustained for a short time and eventually lead to insolvency and closure. The key is to continually monitor the financial health of the company and take action to correct any losses.

We also see many non-accountants promoting the monitoring of cash flow as the key to running a business. While cash flow is important, it is simply a short-term issue. If your debtors increase (because you are poor in collections), of course, cash flow will be an issue. The fix is obvious. If you are losing money, the fix may not be as obvious.

Making a profit must be a strong mindset of the business owner. If they are focused on it, they will make it happen. If they do not focus on it, it can elude them. Running a business requires many skills. Unfortunately, accounting and creativity are mutually exclusive traits. The business owner, if they have trouble focusing on figures or financial matters, should ensure they get help. Business owners who recognise this and get help do well. Those that don't will often fail, as is highlighted by the following example.

We had a client who operated a café in the Blue Mountains in NSW. We had her on Xero and hence could see the weekly and monthly profit and loss statement. There were some timing differences with PAYG and super, but whenever we did the figures, we could see the business was losing money. We did some break-even analysis, but it was always the same. The sales did not cover the food, wages and rent costs. After three months and massive shortfalls, we suggested the client either sell or close. On many occasions, I pointed her to the numbers in Xero, to the net loss the business was showing. I sent her a schedule of the break-even point and what her sales needed to be. She was not prepared to reduce staff or promote the business enough to raise the sales above the break-even point or to even increase prices.

She hated looking at the numbers. She was not very computer literate. She sacrificed all of her savings to prop up the business but it was a lost cause. Eventually, the business was sold for a fraction of what she paid. Many creditors and, of course, the tax office did not get paid. The client had nothing left, so pursuing her personally would have been to no avail.

But, as I have said many times in this book, a business cannot survive for long if it is not making a profit. Know your numbers, monitor your profit and reverse engineer your business to achieve the return you want your business to make. If you cannot run a profitable business, know when it is time to quit. Don't sacrifice all your savings, family money or creditor money on a whim that is not working. Don't waste business oxygen on a failing cause.

26

Money Tip 3:
Pay Yourself First

Anyone who lives within their means
suffers from a lack of imagination.

Oscar Wilde

Having worked with thousands of businesses, it is extremely common for the business owner to ensure all bills are paid before they pay themselves. While this sounds like the right thing to do, in fact, it is counterproductive for the owner. I have seen so many instances where the owner is left with nothing. Over time, a business owner works extremely hard and sacrifices everything. It is soul-destroying. They should reap the benefit of that work, not only *if* the business is a success, but on the way through. It is simply demoralising to live in poverty while you give everything you have to creating your business. So I want to provide some tips on what an entrepreneur must do.

Pay yourself first is the first lesson for a business owner. It forces you to make sure the business makes a profit. In the following chapter, I mention that money is something that sometimes seems to simply evaporate, like water on the footpath. You have all seen it. You have a high bank balance, but yet it seems to just go. I recommend that the best way to handle this is to create several accounts that you set aside. Set aside accounts for taxation, for yourself, for future commitments. You should also use an online saver account. Transfer the money to these accounts and put it away from the business in a difficult place to retrieve. This will force you to focus on creating more money to pay day-to-day bills.

Of course, the owner should not overpay their remuneration. You must always try and keep an eye on profitability and viability, and pay yourself accordingly. Know your own personal KPIs. Know what you want to earn as a fair wage for the work you do. Then pay yourself that wage. Build it into the business overheads to ensure the business can meet this cost. In other words, reverse engineer the break-even point (which will include your personal remuneration) and hence the sales you need to achieve in your business to give you the return you want. If the business cannot sustain this personal remuneration, you need to question whether the business should continue to operate.

The business should deduct tax on this income each week or month as you draw it, and treat yourself and your business as separate entities (which, of course, they are).

On this point, you should continually raise your standards for what you want. I work with many high-net-worth people. They all have high expectations of what they want in life, how they live and the capital they expect (notice I did not say *want* but *expect*) to create. They then make it happen. The raised expectation becomes the new standard. Whenever their income drops below that new standard, they do whatever it takes to ensure they meet this new standard.

Preserving capital is also the key here. I have had some professional gamblers as clients. They never risk their stake or capital. They always keep this safe. They make money, then transfer that profit to real estate or other secure assets. Return *of* capital is always more important than a return *on* capital. Hence, if someone suggests a risky investment that will yield a high rate of return, be careful that the risk and return are directly correlated. The higher the return, the higher the risk. 'If you speculate, it's almost as dangerous if it works than if it doesn't work; you get cocky and take more risks,' said Simon Black, founder of SovereignMan.com.

If you don't set money aside from your business into your own hands, you will find that you are always making excuses that you are investing in your business. While sometimes this may be the case while the business is in its infancy, but you must be realistic, and know when that time has passed. Many times, I have witnessed some unforeseen circumstances occur that can destroy everything. It may not even be something the owner could plan for, like a bushfire, Covid-19 or a global economic collapse. Imagine being at the end of your working life, have sacrificed everything to build a strong and viable business. All your profits were reinvested back into more stock, more infrastructure and growth. Then one of the above occurrences happens and everything is swept away.

Your retirement plans were based on selling a viable and profitable business. Imagine if you were in this situation and you didn't own your own home. If you had not set aside superannuation for retirement. This is why it is important you pay yourself and generate assets in your own name separate to your business.

As mentioned earlier, your business is meant to create life rather than take it away (from you).

27

Money Tip 4:
Set Money Aside

This may sound a strange fact, but the truth is that money does seem to evaporate like water on a footpath. If you leave it unattended or fail to make it work, it just seems to vanish (especially with inflation).

For many people, the more they make, the more they spend. Take Michael Jackson, Elton John, Will Smith, Mike Tyson and many other big names. They all had one thing in common: they were great spenders. It's estimated that by the time of his death, Michael Jackson was $500 million in debt. Mike Tyson blew almost his entire $400 million fortune, and no sooner had Will Smith made his first million, he had spent his first $2 million. Sounds crazy, but it is true. These spending habits are not unique to famous people. I have seen it with many clients. I have clients who are doctors, lawyers and even high-earning entrepreneurs. They are always matching their lifestyle to their income or perceived income. No matter how much comes in, they just never put any of it away. It's almost like they make sure there's never anything left over. Of course, they forget about tax. Five years pass. Then 10. Then 20, and suddenly, before they know it, they are 60 years old with nothing to show for all their hard work. Many people don't get it. Most people think it's all about how much you can bring in. How much you fill your wallet. But there's more to it than that. Earl Nightingale, in one of his famous short speeches, called this the 'strangest secret', and that 95 per cent of the population will retire broke. This was in 1956.

What actually happens is that you find things to spend money on. Most people are not good savers; they are followers. They follow the trends of the poor. When their bank balance is high, they tend to spend it on the latest new item: a new house, new car, new clothes. They are victims of an overload of advertising and the peer pressure of living in a consumer age. They have not been educated on how to create and keep wealth. Sadly, schools have a lot to answer for on this. Then when bills come along later, like GST or other taxes, they don't have the money to pay it. So they borrow it. Then they borrow more to buy a new car or house, thinking they are making the money so it will not be an issue. In *Rich Dad Poor Dad*, Robert Kiyosaki talks about good debt and bad debt. About creating wealth first, then spending it. About not borrowing money for consumables that depreciate. If this is a problem you have, I suggest you read this book.

A high bank balance is often a timing issue and not a reflection of profitability. Depending on the business you operate, sometimes cash flow can be good at certain cycles and then poor. Hence, you need to manage the ebbs and flows.

As mentioned in an earlier chapter, the solution to this is simple. Create separate bank accounts from your normal trading account. With internet banking, it is easy to transfer between different accounts. Then reduce your trading account to a small balance to cover the normal expenses. Say, about two weeks cash flow. Set aside surplus funds into the business online saver account. This set aside money will be used for those things that may come back to bite you, like : taxes, bank loans, staff super and PAYG. Items that need to be paid that will cause grief if they are not paid.

Firstly, it gives you security because you know you have the funds available to meet these commitments, and secondly, it forces you to dig deep and create more. If you forget about the set aside balance and focus on building back the trading account balance, it has the effect of making you create more. The pressure makes you find that extra sale, collect that amount owing; this might make you excel at creating solutions, at manifesting a way through. Some people need this pressure (or even the pressure of failure) to make a solution happen. All business owners have this power. Learn how to focus on using it to create wealth.

28

Money Tip 5: How Tax Works and How to Use It to Create Wealth

*Money may not buy happiness but
it sure beats being poor.*
Various Authors

The following is an extract from my book *How to Choose an Accountant* (edited, of course).

To understand how to reduce your tax, it is first necessary to understand the taxation system. When that is understood, you will be able to work the system to your advantage. This is what every wealthy person does, and it is one of the ways they become even wealthier. In my time at Consolidated Press Holdings, Kerry Packer was a master at it. I have since used it to compound my wealth. When I had farming operations, they were a drain on my finances, health and time. However, I carried forward large tax losses that helped me reduce my tax for many years, thanks to Mr Keating, who changed the system to allow carried forward losses to be carried forward indefinitely (previously it was only seven years). Again, it is about knowing how to use the system to your advantage.

Taxation can be likened to a cost. You often hear the expression 'the taxation office is your silent partner'. With tax rates for individuals topping 48.5 per cent and for company's 25–30 per cent, this is easy to understand.

We all want to reduce our tax, but before we get carried away with simple cost-cutting measures, it is important to understand some fundamentals about money, income and tax.

We all need money to survive, prosper and grow. Money gives you the ability to make choices. It gives you the freedom and the wherewithal to help others. The basis of happiness is productivity, not money. Money is the means of exchange for that production. An abundance of money means an abundance of products being given or exchanged. The result will be high morale and happiness. If you disagree with this, talk to an unemployed person who is idle all day. They are the unhappiest members of society. Hence, if you want to help your family, friends and society, you need to be able to work and produce, and keep as much of that production to disburse as you wish.

However, the problem is that our system does not encourage this. A person who relies on a job for his or her sole income is disadvantaged under our current taxation system. An employee is taxed first and spends what is left, whereas an investor or business person is taxed last.

> To create wealth, you must be either
> an investor or be in business.

Let me cover this point again, as it is so important to grasp. If you earn your income from your business or from property or share investments, all of your expenses are offset against this income. If you buy more property or more business assets, all borrowing costs, depreciation and any other costs will reduce the amount on which you pay tax. You then pay tax on the balance. However, as an employee, you pay your tax each week first. You can't even claim the cost of travel to your workplace.

This is made clearer in the table below:

Figure 14 Simple Tax Structure

	Salary earner	Business Owner (company structure)
Income	120,000	120,000
Business expenses		55,000
Tax payable	29,467	17,875
Medicare levy	2400	
Medicare levy surcharge	1500	
Total tax	33,367	17,875
Money left	86,633	102,125

The effect of the above is that the salary earner has less money available to use to build assets for wealth creation. This keeps an employee reliant on an employer for income. It is difficult for an employee to save the capital required to break free from this cycle. In the previous section, I mentioned how sometimes people can be suppressed, by the system or the taxation office itself. If you can recognise this source of suppression, you are better positioned to overcome it.

As mentioned, you must aim to earn as much income as possible. You must *never* spend money in order to simply get a taxation deduction. This is crazy logic. Many people invest in tax schemes or tax minimisation strategies simply because of the tax benefit. These include agricultural managed investments or other tax schemes that promise long-term growth for upfront deductions. Some of these have been made illegal, with investors being forced to pay back the tax involved. Most fail to earn anything like the income they promised and generally result in a loss of the money invested. Do not get caught up by these schemes. Remember, if it sounds too good to be true, it probably isn't true.

The next step is to keep as much of that income as possible. This is almost the most important part. It doesn't matter how much money you make; it is how much you keep that is important.

This is where tax reduction is vital. As stated earlier, your silent partner, the taxation office, will demand and take (without your permission) up to 48.5 per cent if employed and 25–30 per cent if you operate through a company. That is the law. As mentioned, if you are an employee, they will take it first, before you buy your shopping, pay your mortgage or feed your family. I bet you have never thought of tax like this before. It is an interesting way to look at the matter.

In the table above, both earned $120,000. However, the person in business had $102,125 left, whereas the employee had only $86,633. The business owner invested $55,000 in business expenses. This may help grow the business and make more money next year. In other words, build wealth. The salary earner made no such investments.

The solution is to reduce your tax legally. Let me say firmly at this point that it must be legal. Using illegal methods is non-survival and will come back to bite you.

This involves taking advantage of the system and its benefits. Taxation has always had built-in incentives to help businesses grow and to employ people. The history of taxation and its complicated structure evolved from these incentives, which became loopholes, which were then exploited. The game for accountants and tax lawyers has always been to find the loopholes and exploit them before they are closed.

Taxation laws in Australia consist of over 100,000 pages of legislation, rulings and regulations. Many are contradictory and many leave themselves open to interpretation. You often see press releases where the Australian Taxation Office is taking a company to court over alleged tax evasion. The company, which has engaged the best and most highly paid accountants and tax lawyers, will say they have done nothing wrong. The taxation office has a different view. Hence, it is not as clear cut as many would have you believe.

However, there are two things you can do if you are in business or an investor, and these will dramatically limit the amount of tax you pay. This will give you more money available to invest further to increase your future income with the ultimate aim of building wealth. Firstly, you must consider your tax structure. As you can see from the previous example, this can reduce your tax dramatically. Secondly, you must consider investing money for your future in tax-deductible expenditure. For a business investor, this is easy. For an employee, it is almost impossible. As mentioned earlier, to save tax and build wealth, you must be either an investor or in business.

The tax rates for various structures are as below:

Figure 15 Australian Resident Tax Rates 2021–22 (individuals)

Taxable income	Tax on this income
0–$18,200	Nil
$18,201–$45,000	19c for each $1 over $18,200
$45,001–$120,000	$5092 plus 32.5c for each $1 over $45,000
$120,001–$180,000	$29,467 plus 37c for each $1 over $120,000
$180,001 and over	$51,667 plus 45c for each $1 over $180,000

Source: ATO website, https://www.ato.gov.au/rates/individual-income-tax-rates/
The above rates do not include the Medicare levy of 2 per cent.

Figure 16 Company Tax Rates 2021–22

Income category	Rate (%)
Base rate entities – 2021	26
Base rate entities – 2022	25
Otherwise	30

Note: This includes corporate limited partnerships, strata title bodies corporate, trustees of corporate unit trusts and public trading trusts. Refer to Chapter 6 on tax rates for different entities for a full description of the manner in which companies are taxed.

Source: ATO website, https://www.ato.gov.au/Rates/Changes-to-company-tax-rates/

Figure 17 Complying Superannuation Funds Tax Rates 2021–22

Income category of fund	Rate (%)
In pension mode	0
In accumulation mode	15

Note: The income earned by a superannuation fund can be a mix of pension mode and accumulation mode. It is based on the members of the fund and their situation. For example, if all members are in pension mode and their balance is below the balance transfer cap.

Source: ATO website, https://www.ato.gov.au/Super/Self-managed-super-funds/Investing/Tax-on-income/

Figure 18 Trusts: Discretionary and Fixed Trusts Tax Rates

Income category	Rate (%)
If all income is distributed to beneficiaries or unit holders	0
If no beneficiary is presently entitled to the income	45

Note: Before 30 June each year, the trust must elect to whom it will distribute its net profit. Providing all profit is distributed, no tax is payable by the trustee.

Source: ATO website, https://www.ato.gov.au/general/trusts/trust-income/

It doesn't take a genius to look at the above tables and consider how best to use the system to minimise your tax. Generally, with a mix of the above, plus a few other tricks that most accountants have up their sleeve, a person's contribution to consolidated revenue can be lessened.

You must plan. You must be in control of where you are heading.

This is where a good accountant will be worth far more than what he or she costs. A first-class accountant is your secret weapon to financial success.

29

Money Tip 6: Calculating Your Net Worth

Many of us only ever calculate our net worth when we are applying for a loan. The bank asks us to present a personal balance sheet showing all our assets and liabilities. It is then promptly forgotten. I bet if I challenged you now, you could not, off the top of your head, tell me your net worth within a 10 per cent margin.

Generally, your financial life is complicated. You have businesses, property and loans that vary dramatically from time to time. Shares can change daily. Your super fund balance moves every payday, your car loans and credit card loans change constantly, depending on what day of the month it is.

Life is too short to spend it always counting your money. But your wealth does fluctuate. The more you have invested, the more these fluctuations occur. They are not something you need to worry about, but you cannot hide your head in the sand either.

I therefore suggest you do a six-month check on your net worth – taking stock of your current assets minus liabilities – as this can yield valuable information about your financial health. It will help you see if you are having trouble servicing your debt or if your debt is hindering your ability to save. It will also help you plan for that day when you will no longer be earning income but need to live off your accumulated assets (ie retirement). It can help to ensure you have a good spread of assets across a number of sectors and are well diversified.

Creating a statement of your net worth is an ideal starting point for determining your financial priorities.

A very important part of calculating your net worth is that it will give you a six-monthly comparison from last year and a basis for future planning. How many people say they want to retire by, say, 50 but never sit down and work out how they will do that? They never quantify what net worth they need to retire on.

Listed below is a simple example of a net worth calculation. You may need to print it or create your own net worth spreadsheet. You can save your net worth statement as either a printout or an electronic document.

As stated above, you should do this every six months. For example, on 31 December and 30 June. Then compare the net worth figure. Hopefully, it will have increased. If not, you need to take action to fix this.

Below are the things to collate to work out your net worth.

Step 1: Document Your Assets

Take stock of your net worth by putting together your most recent investment statements or going online to retrieve your current account balances. For some accounts, such as your bank account, share trading accounts or superannuation accounts, you should be able to get a very current, very specific value on those assets. Don't forget your superannuation fund balances. People often miss this because it is not top of mind. For other assets, such as the value of your home and car, you'll need to make an educated guess. With your car, you can search online to find its value.

List out the following assets:

- Cash account balances – your cheque and savings account balances.
- Superannuation fund balances.
- Life insurance policy face value.
- Current market value of your home and any investment properties. Be realistic. Inflation is often a problem when we self-assess our home's value.
- Estimate of the current market value of other assets, including cars, jewellery, artwork, and so on. (Again, be realistic; tangible property isn't often worth what we think it is). Make a list.
- Any other assets that have financial value, like your business. For a business, it will depend on the industry. A rule of thumb for a small business will be either 9 to 12 months turnover, if in professional services or real estate. For other businesses, the value will be a multiple of net earnings before interest, tax, depreciation and amortisation (EBITDA). This multiple will be from three to five times EBITDA. Pick an earnings multiple and stick to it.

Step 2: Document Your Liabilities

On the liabilities side of your net worth, make a list of all outstanding debts. These will include the following:

- mortgage loan balances
- home equity loan, home equity line of credit, reverse mortgage (only document if you currently have a balance)
- HECS loan
- credit card debt
- car loan
- any other debt

Step 3: Calculate and Analyse Net Worth

Now that you have listed all of your assets and liabilities, you can calculate your net worth. Subtract the liabilities from the assets. Hopefully, you will be left with a positive number. If not, you have real problems.

Now comes the fun. Look at this honestly and realistically. Then ask yourself:

- Is my net worth in the red or just barely positive? If so, you've got some work to do. In earlier chapters, we discussed knowing your numbers. Set a budget for where you want to be in five or ten years' time.
- Is my net worth in great shape? Is it what I have been aiming for? Something I can be proud of? Just be careful not to let the 'wealth effect' go to your head. Not only has the economy been strong and unemployment low, but the stock market has been on an extended growth, pumping up the net worth of anyone who holds stocks or stock funds in their portfolios. Be realistic and consider how wealthy you would feel if your portfolio lost 10 per cent, 20 per cent or even more. Such losses have been commonplace in stock market history; in the most recent downturn, 2007–2009, stocks lost 56 per cent of their value from peak to trough.

Step 4: Compare Your Net Worth against Last Year

If you calculate your net worth every six months, on 30 June and on 31 December each year, you have fixed dates to compare against. Then you can really see the effect of time and how well your plans are going. It also helps iron out any unusual occurrences, like a stock market boom/crash or a property boom/slump.

Ask yourself:

- How does my net worth compare with what it was at this time last year?
- How does my current debt load compare with what it was a year ago?
- Do I have a spread of investments or assets such that no one asset is a disproportionate share of my net worth, for instance, a large exposure to one sector of the stock market, or a heavy concentration in residential or commercial real estate? Such heavy concentrations can leave you exposed to risk. There is also a risk if they're not very liquid, such as real estate.
- Are all of my assets adequately insured? Don't just consider assets like your home and car, but your human capital, which you can insure with disability and life insurance.
- If you are still working, do you have enough liquid assets in place to cover your living expenses for six months or more? This is just in case you get retrenched, your business fails or some other event happens that causes your income to stop.
- If you're retired, do you have enough assets in highly liquid investments to cover expenses for two years, as well as any emergencies or home and car repairs?
- If you're getting close to retirement, is your current net worth on track to supply you with the living expenses you need, in addition to whatever you'll receive from a pension?

The above are simple questions that every person needs to answer. As mentioned a number of times, unfortunately, 95 per cent of the population retires broke. Why? Because they, like sheep, follow the masses and never plan for their retirement. They live for today, listen to the media on what has happened, and follow the masses by selling when everyone else sells, buying when everyone else buys, and generally mistiming most aspects of the market. By retiring broke, I mean that they do not have enough money to live without some form of assistance when they retire. This assistance may be from family, the government or charity.

I remember Kerry Packer, as chairman and the major shareholder of Australian Consolidated Press Limited (ACP), saying in a board meeting that if everyone was buying, that was the time to sell. He had an uncanny way of knowing when to swim against the tide. When Alan Bond (Bond Corporation) offered to buy Channel 9 from ACP for just over $1 billion in 1987, Kerry said it was an offer he could not refuse. He hated selling Channel 9 and it really left a hole in the business. But $1 billion buys a lot of hole filling. Timing was everything. At that time, the share market was at an all-time high. Needless to say, after that boom, there was a massive bust, but not for Kerry. Bond Corporation did not pay the $400 million balance it owed, so ACP took back Channel 9. The $600 million that they received upfront was forfeited by Bond Corporation.

In another example, in 1992, Westpac was experiencing some massive debt write-offs. Their shares dropped to just under $3. I remember playing golf at Manly Golf Club at the time and walking down the ninth fairway talking about it. One of my golf partners was complaining that Kerry pushed the price up to over $3.20 by being a buyer. He sold that parcel about a year later to Lend Lease, making over $100 million in profit. He later bought them back, selling them again for a huge profit.

Your motto should be: do not follow the sheep over the edge of the cliff. Keep money aside and take your own counsel on what to do. In the case of small business owners, keep money aside.

Purchase assets and put money into superannuation or other assets for your future needs. Follow what Kerry did – not what everyone does. If you are in a boom market, know that, by nature, booms and recessions can be cyclical.

30

Money Tip 7: Using Other People's Money

Using other people's money (OPM) really means gearing, using money in the most effective way to multiply your return. It makes sense to borrow, or use other people's money, if you can earn a higher rate than the cost of that money, money which you may not have personally. It makes business sense to go down that path. But be cautious of risk. In an earlier chapter, I covered what compounding means and the ability to grow your assets exponentially. OPM does exactly that. By being clever, you can create extraordinary wealth by finding opportunities and selling that idea to others who can share in some of that gain. I have seen many entrepreneurs do exactly that. They make money out of an idea, and some even make extraordinary gains.

Let me focus on property first, as it is a little easier to explain in numbers. However, the same holds true for loans to acquire a business or stock that you sell.

In the early 1900s, many people bought houses or other assets with cash. They did not use a bank or financial institution. However, this was a time when house prices were around a year's wages, so that was possible. Now, with house prices in Sydney being nearly 10 times average earnings, this is far more difficult. Hence, you must borrow from a bank or financial institution to do so. This makes sense.

If the price of property increases over time, more than the interest you pay, then you are in front. Let's say the bank will provide a loan at 3 per cent p.a. If property prices increase by more than this amount, you are in front. Of course, you need to factor in, on the negative side, your holding costs; and, on the positive side, any rent received, or if you live in the property, the costs of your personal housing. Also factor in your ability to service any debt.

Using simple mathematics, if you have a $5 million property portfolio that is 100 per cent geared at, say, 3 per cent, you can assume the rents or tax relief will cover the interest costs. If you hold that property portfolio for 10 years, you could expect it to be worth $10 million. You will owe the bank $5 million, which can easily be repaid by selling half of your portfolio. Hence, using other people's money has just made you $5 million. This is, of course, very simplistic. But there are many, many stories of people who have done exactly that. Timing is important and ensuring you can service the above is also vital. The example shows how using other people's money allows you to build wealth, creating $5 million. But be certain that if you follow this strategy that you can weather any ups and downs, that the income received will cover all interest costs. During the global financial crisis, many people lost everything because they could not meet their holding costs. The unfortunate part is that if they had been able to hold their investments, they would have more than doubled their gain.

Another example is using an options or extended settlement. Sometimes, a great property comes up that is underpriced. Banks often enter as mortgagee in possession and want to offload a property. Sometimes a seller simply wants out. With a little work, you can improve its value. So, you enter into an option for say six months or request an extended settlement date. In the contract, you ensure that you have the right to occupy and to work on the property from the date the contract is executed. During this time, you renovate the property and have it ready for re-sale before settlement. You then re-advertise it at a higher price. I have seen clients do exactly this. You have a buyer on settlement and do the purchase and sale at the same time and walk away with the profit. The only money down is the deposit and renovation cost. You walk away with a healthy profit.

Many people do the same with development sites. They enter into an option at a price, arrange for a DA for a change of use to build a duplex or some other change, then sell it on at a profit before they have even purchased. Developers do this all the time.

The same holds true for business. Putting aside for a moment the business risk, if you buy a business with a bank loan at, say, 6 per cent, and the business earns both a return for yourself and repays the loan, then you have again created wealth.

I stress, however, that there is a practical side to acquiring property or acquiring a business that is outside the scope of this book.

My point is: do not be afraid of income-related debt. When used effectively, it can be a powerful wealth creation tool. Using other people's money, from a bank or a private lender, can be a powerful tool that, when handled with care, can make you extremely wealthy.

31

Money Tip 8: Your Road to Riches

In this chapter I will bring together all of the previous Money Tip chapters and explain in a very simple way how to build great wealth. While this book is not intended as a financial planning book, I would be doing my clients and readers a disservice if I did not pass on my many years of wisdom, the trial-and-error lessons learned from a life in the financial world.

Before I get to the meat in the sandwich, I want to discuss why it is important to plan ahead and how this philosophical strategy works. It is what most people who have wealth have done, even though they don't realise it. Yes, there are those who have created a massive business. But the average wealthy person has followed the strategy listed below. Even those who are employed have done this, though these people do not have the advantages of those who are in business and hence cannot use the tax system the way business owners can.

Let me talk about the landscape first. You work or run a business. The ATO takes about a third to half, so the balance is what you have left to deal with. So to build wealth you need to follow a saving pattern to give you a deposit or somehow take a leap of faith and borrow to the hilt. In other words, you use other people's money, gearing or prepayments to give you a tax refund boost and all the things mentioned earlier in the chapter. Now comes the tricky part. The part that no one tells you about. That is, luck and timing. People tell you how smart they are with investing and so on, but in most cases there is an element of luck. In truth, you cannot predict the economy. You cannot predict a recession, pandemic or financial crisis. So you need to be careful. If you take the above path and the economy throws you a curve ball, stand up and dust yourself off and try again. It happens. It doesn't always happen and is perhaps a once in a five or ten year event. Step back and do it again. Don't be disillusioned and throw the towel into the ring.

So now I have dealt with the negative, the reality of life and why some people trip over and never pick themselves up. However, those who are lucky enough to not trip, who are able to time the first couple of foundation building steps, never look back.

Let me now cover the true message of this chapter with a simple example that will explain what most people actually have done to create wealth. Believe me, it is not rocket science.

Let us assume that you are out to create a $10 million portfolio. It doesn't matter whether it is shares or property, but it is an asset portfolio whose past history tells you it will increase and be stable and income earning. And the income earned will cover any holding costs. So let's use property as that is an easy item to visualise. But I have seen people do it with share portfolios. Every year they buy more and more blue chip shares like Commonwealth Bank or BHP. Remember the example in the Chapter 19, where Mrs G did this for 30 years and now has a portfolio that is worth in excess of $7 million with a cost base of $2 million, and earns $300,000 p.a. in dividends, mostly franked.

The strategy is simple with the steps as below:

- Firstly, it doesn't matter how much borrowing you have as long as the income covers the interest and repayments. Or you can structure the asset that way. Remember, the bigger the base, the larger the gains will be due to asset growth, inflation, etc.

- Assume that in some years using the gross asset base of $10 million, it grows 3 per cent – that's a gain of $300,000 for doing nothing.
- In some years you will get a 5 to 8 per cent increase; now you have made $500,000 to $800,000. In a 10-year period there will be a great year where the returns will be 20 per cent. There may be a road bump where the value drops. But if you look at any chart, even over the past 100 years, the trend will always be up.
- Compounding the above, in five years your asset base should grow by about 50 per cent, or in my example, above $5,000,000. If you have debt, you may wish to sell down some assets to reduce it, but maybe not. When you sell to pay down debt you crystallise a capital gain and there will be tax consequences. The smart thing to do is to use the increased equity to increase your asset base. The important part is having a large enough asset pool or base that a small increase will give you massive returns. Hence 5 per cent on $10 million will give you a $500,000 gain or a $500,000 income, if you look at it that way. An unrealised and hence tax-free gain.
- Be clever about selling down as tax will not be your friend here. Use the CGT concessions and prepayment rules to their max. But hopefully you will have amassed enough wealth that you do not care.
- I guarantee you, barring a recession in the middle, if you hold this course your $10 million geared property or share portfolio will turn in a $10 million net worth. You will never need to work again and reap the benefits.

So how do you create the above $10 million portfolio? Firstly, you do it a year at a time. Every year you buy an asset, which will be geared maybe to 80 per cent. Use the tax system to help you as covered elsewhere in this book. How do you fund the first purchase? This is the hardest step. It will be what differentiates you, the future wealth builder, from the average person who talks but never acts. The person who others will envy and say you are just lucky. So save, scrimp, get help, find a way and do it. Borrow on your house, do what it takes. Then, over the next five years, you continue purchasing and don't sell. You may hit some roadblocks or poor timing issues, but in time these will sort themselves out. Look back and you can see that with every bump in the road, there were smooth waters ahead. Hold your cool.

I know you are thinking this looks easy so why doesn't everybody do it? I can tell you firstly a lot of people do exactly this. They don't brag and tell others, except their accountants (me) so I see it, I know. They have that quiet financially independent smile on their face. Life is now easy for them.

A word of warning, don't let yourself be talked into buying overpriced assets. Take off any rose-coloured glasses. Watch out for the so-called financial advisors who are trying to sell you overpriced property that earns them a massive commission. Don't buy shares at the top of the market when the index is overheated. Don't rush, but don't sit on the fence either. Do your homework and be intelligent about what you buy. But also act. Timing and holding onto assets for a long period will always be your friend.

So why doesn't everybody follow this strategy? Some are simply afraid to step outside their comfort zone. They follow the masses who do not think intelligently. They talk to the wrong people. Have the wrong financial mentors, do not read self-help books, do not invest in their own financial education and then complain why they are poor. Then they justify their poor life strategy by telling others that we are all meant to live in poverty. They follow those who hit a road bump on the way and have let themselves sink into depression and a 'poor me' type financial attitude. They have become suppressed by the system and never recovered. Read Chapter 38, 'Millionaire Mindset' and you can see how this can happen. If this is you, isn't it time to change? To rethink your assumptions about life and wealth?

If you want to create your own life of abundance, do what the wealthy do. These are the self-funded retirees that you never hear about. They quietly get on with life, drive their nice cars, have nice motor homes and travel the country. They quietly tell the government what they can do with their 10 cent pensions and go about living a life in the manner that we all aspire to.

Simple but a reality.

Part 5

Success in Business – Physical, Psychological and Emotional Aspects

In this section, I will cover the true cost of creating a business, the ups and the downs of success or failure. Unfortunately, it is a fact that the difference between succeeding and failing can be very minor. Like the roll of a dice, it can be a pandemic, a recession, poor timing, a change in the property market or a change of bank manager causing a loan to be called in. Things that are sometimes outside the business owner's control. Bob Proctor states that the difference between success and failure sometimes can be as minor as a 6 per cent shift.

Unfortunately, I have seen both successes and failures with clients, and the true cost of both. One day, a rooster; the next day, a feather duster; one day, valued news; the next day, wrapping paper for garbage.

All businesses are created by a person with single-minded determination. One person's dream creates a reality that grows, prospers or fails based on the founder's ability to bring those dreams into reality. Every business is created that way. A person has a dream (or sees a need), and with single-minded determination works to achieve that dream.

But in doing so, there is a cost. A cost not measured in dollars and cents but in emotional ways. Sometimes that cost will be too great to bear. It can result in the downfall of the dreamer. It is this passion – this determination – that sets the business owner apart from others in society, those who are simply willing to accept the status quo, the employees, the public servants in society.

The costs of entrepreneurship may yield massive rewards, like the Elon Musks or Richard Bransons of this world. Or they may yield high personal failure, like Alan Bond, who went to prison, or Rene Rivkin, the flamboyant stock trader who took his own life in May 2005. But there is no escaping the psychological and emotional side of the path the business owner or entrepreneur has taken, a toll that may lead to massive success or massive failure.

Before you embark on this journey, consider what it takes. Many do not. Think about the education that is needed, the knowledge you must acquire. The ups and downs that may follow. Many see the successes, which are widely reported, but not the failures. Enter this road with your eyes open to the true cost of this journey.

In this section, I will cover the other side of business: the self-help, emotional strength and power that entrepreneurs have. The non-financial side. On the one hand, entrepreneurs have the power to bring into their life the things they need to succeed, but on the other, they also need to recognise the aspects of what it takes to succeed and what to do when outside factors thwart that success.

32

Ethics and Business

This may seem a strange topic for an analytical tax and business book, however, it is true that to be successful, you need to be on the right side of the law. This book deals with using the tax system to your advantage, but it never advises you to cheat or evade taxation. That would be breaking the law.

I also take this point further from an ethical point of view. If you are a business owner, or simply a person trying to succeed in life, being a harsh or difficult person, besides not winning friends and influencing people, will have an effect on your success. The same applies if your moral compass is distorted. Such people, if they have some success, generally lose it. For example, in the entertainment industry, generally, it's the person who integrates extremely well and is liked by everyone who does well. There are many examples where skills, acting ability and looks are all similar, yet the one who excels is the one people relate to and want to help. The same applies in business. Staff will not respect you or help you, and your competitors will work against you and generally put you down if you are unethical or you are not a nice person to work with.

This does not mean you will be soft, a pushover or allow people to use you. You can be a hard businessperson but still be respectful of others and your team. Kerry Packer was always respectful, and the same applies for the number of other high-net-worth clients I currently look after.

In my view, if your ethics are out of line, it is hard to succeed. Remember, a business is a manifestation of the owner of the business. 'The fish stinks from the head down' is as true today as it was when the expression was coined. It means that when a company is struggling, the likely cause comes from the owner. It also means that a company is a reflection of its owners and leaders. It will generally be in line with those people's ethical and moral values.

Companies or business owners who cheat the system, do not pay their staff the correct wages, have no regard for the environment or cheat on their taxes will eventually be found out and shamed. Companies that have a distorted social and moral compass in today's world generally fail.

I think the reason behind this is that most people are basically good, and if you dig deep enough, we find that most people are well-intentioned. Being basically good, people who do the wrong thing tend to self-sabotage themselves to subconsciously punish their wrong actions. They even subconsciously destroy their business because of this innate push to rectify any unethical behaviour. Hence, in my view, a key factor in making yourself and your business a success is to have a strong moral compass.

I use the words *business* and *yourself* interchangeably because for the entrepreneur, their business is their life. Their business is a manifestation of the business owner or entrepreneur.

The public demands nothing less from its leaders. Make no mistake, an entrepreneur is a leader in business who in turn creates employment, a better economy and improves the lives of those around them. The key factor is succeeding, because if you do not succeed, you cannot achieve the above. A vibrant and solid economy requires entrepreneurs to take a risk to grow, to build businesses and create employment. It requires the private sector to do this and be supported by government by creating the right framework.

At a micro level, it is you, the entrepreneur, who is so important to the economy and to the world. You have an obligation to get it right, as in any economy, there are only a few leaders, a few successful people, a few true entrepreneurs to achieve this aim. The rest of the population is evolving at a different level.

33

Some People Can Drag Your Business Down

If everyone is moving forward together,
then success takes care of itself.

Henry Ford

No book on the keys to operating a successful business would be complete without an outline of a key component that can drag a business down: people.

A good example of this exact problem was a client I had when I had my accounting practice on the NSW Central Coast. In about 2009, a client who installed solar panels came to me for help. He was in a business that, at the time, metaphorically, had a licence to print money. But he wasn't doing well. I could see there were some personal issues that were affecting him but couldn't put my finger on it. I asked him to have his key staff tested so I could try to find the intangible problem in his business. Quite simply, he had two key staff members who were bringing him down. He dealt with one but would not deal with the other. He was too nice. This person was a suppressive and continually worked against the business aims. To his face, she was all nice, but deep down, she worked to subconsciously sabotage his business. I don't think she even knew she was doing it. Eventually, the business lost all key contracts, shrunk to a non-viable level and went into liquidation. I could see it, but the client couldn't. I was pleased when they went elsewhere.

In my book *Business Bullseye,* I wrote a chapter on understanding people. Originally, I titled it 'The good, the bad and the ugly'. My editor at the time said I could not say that and we agreed on 'The good, the bad and the indolent'. By ugly, I didn't mean physically but psychologically bad. There are people in this world who are not nice people. They will murder, maim and destroy others without any compassion. They are the narcissistic, the Hitlers of this world. According to Freud, they make up about 5 per cent of the population. They have no empathy. They will take from you everything you own and leave you destitute. Frankly, they are people you do not want around you. Sometimes they put up a nice facade and will be difficult to spot.

Then there is another approximately 22 per cent who are under the spell of these narcissistic people. They are suppressed in life. They are controlled at an emotional level to the point that their life is always a mixture of problems. You know these people because you are always making excuses for them. They are always having accidents, are always sick or are always late. They seem to bring problems with them wherever they go.

Be aware that both people exist, and if you can identify these patterns, you can ensure you are not affected by these narcissistic people or those who are suppressed by them. Get both personality types out of your life. It is not your job to rehabilitate them. Move them on. My solar client didn't and suffered the consequences. He was fooled, kept his rose-coloured glasses on and would not confront the issue. Failure to confront is a big problem in business, and business owners must step up to the plate, take responsibility and act.

So let me reiterate the things you need to look out for and how to spot them. After all, to be a success, you cannot have people in your business and your life, for that matter, who work against you or are not on your team. We all know that everyone is different. We all have different experiences in life, different aspirations and different desires. This is what makes a country great. Listed below are some examples of the differences. Remember, you as a business owner will be dependent on people to assist you achieve your business goals. You cannot do it alone. You must assemble and lead a team to fulfil the aims of the business. So you need to become an expert in people and psychology. This will alert you to those you need to move away from, as mentioned earlier in this chapter, but also to those you choose to allow to remain part of your team.

Truths about People and How to Deal with Them

- **People often prefer the fake versions of us, depending upon whether we naturally have an agreeable personality or not.** As children, we are encouraged to be ourselves. As adults, we certainly can do this, but if we do, we can't expect others to always like us. We may lose friends, career promotions and be alienated from family. A person who is narcissistic will soon learn how to hide their true self. They will learn what fake version of themselves will be socially acceptable to achieve their aims. A suppressive will know how to make you feel sorry for them and hence want to try and help them. Don't be fooled by the wolf in sheep's clothing.
- **You cannot trust your children with strangers, or even members of your own family.** Always be alert and watchful of signs. The Boy Scouts of America went bankrupt and dissolved due to lawsuits based on tens of thousands of incidents of sexual abuse of young boys. Paedophile priests and pastors ran rampant in the Catholic Church for decades.

- **There are some people who are dead inside.** There is no hidden good person inside of them. You can sometimes see it in their eyes. These people often turn out to be the rapists, murderers and violent criminals in our society. They are people with no empathy.
- **Many people cannot grasp the absurdity of the rat race until they have completed the maze.** In other words, they can be trusting to the point of naivety. Don't allow yourself to be a victim of one of these people.
- **So many years and tears are wasted trying to 'resolve' differences that have nothing to do with your actions.** A scapegoat hasn't 'done' anything. They are victims of an unwinnable lottery. If you are a scapegoat in your family, nothing you say or do can change that. You cannot 'work out your differences', 'lay out your heart' and have it change anything. In fact, people will use your vulnerabilities against you. There is only one solution: get out and don't look back.
- **People are different and have innate traits that you cannot change.** As a parent, you see the enormous power of genetics. Parents help nurture their children, but 80 per cent of who we are is the product of a random combination of genes. A set of fraternal twins might as well be from different planets, with their looks, height, intelligence, hair colour and interests all radically different. Studies of identical twins reared apart show the huge influence of genes on several aspects of our personality, intelligence, height, preferences, and so on.
- **One man's heaven is another man's hell.** People see things differently and live different lives, even in the same environment. Their inner workings are simply tuned differently.

- **Trust your gut.** It usually ends up being right, but you only realise this after you ignore it and give a shady person your trust. Intuitively, you often know what to do, but sometimes you allow that false facade of the person to influence you; to blind you. When you are outside of that person's influence, you know what to do. Then, when you are back within their environment, you are fooled again. Follow your gut feeling.
- **Everything is politics – even your family.** You can be the most competent person in the world, but if you aren't political, you will be passed over, bullied or ignored. So understand that sometimes you need to have an opinion, a cause or something you believe in. Then study it and be prepared to defend your beliefs. Do not let yourself be bullied into acquiescing to someone else's cause or someone else's political agenda.
- **The strongest form of violence is often mass quiet assent.** This was the case in Germany during the Second World War, when people called for their Jewish neighbours to be arrested and taken to concentration camps. While survival is important and taking survival decisions vital, don't be prepared to accept things that are outside your personal ethics. Stand up for yourself, have an opinion and act on that opinion. In America, where voting is not compulsory, only one-third of the population votes. The rest either accept the status quo or do nothing about it. If you want the leader who will serve your country best, then vote. Don't sit quietly in a corner and then complain later.

In building your team, be aware of the intangible aspects of people. Understand the above traits. Recognise the backstabbers, the thieves, the dishonest, the narcissistic, the suppressive, the people who have a facade that hides their true self. They will destroy your business. Learn to know the difference between those people and the people you want in your life. There are good people out there who are willing to help or have the same objective you have, but don't be naive enough to think everyone is in that category. Do not hesitate to sack anyone whose objectives are not in alignment with yours. But, more importantly, be intelligent about how you guide your business and yourself to prosperity.

34

The Psychological Price of Entrepreneurship

Building a business is not an easy task. In reality, it can be difficult and at times very hard, especially if uncontrolled events happen. We have clients whose businesses, because of Covid-19, are totally decimated. One faces losing everything, including their home of 30 years. No one could have predicted the events of the last two years, yet these entrepreneurs must now deal with it. Business owners who create a business pay a hefty price for the passion and drive that led them to create their business. If things go wrong, it is a price that they often bear in private – often they will only confide in their accountant on these close and personally confronting issues. To truly understand the demons these people face, the following is a real-life example of what I have seen occur (changed to protect the business owner it related to).

Consider 'Bill', a fictional lawyer and partner in a large legal practice in the city. He also has some clients he looks after privately. Bill helps clients with their legal matters, attends court, sets up complicated infrastructure deals and constantly travels to China on business. As a lawyer, his charges are based on time, hence to recover high fees he needs to work extremely long hours. He is often going home late, seeing clients or attending networking activities on the way home. Back in 2008, Bill was working long hours counselling nervous clients about getting out of debt, helping them decide if they should enter bankruptcy. But his calm demeanour masked a secret: He shared their fears. Like them, Bill was sinking deeper and deeper into debt. He had driven himself far into the red starting from a short-term, high-interest, non-traditional lender. He was hearing how depressed and strung out his clients were, but in the back of his mind, he was thinking, 'I've got twice as much debt as you do.'

He had illegally cashed in his superannuation fund and maxed out his credit cards, applying for more credit when he was sent a new card with an interest-free period. He was up to over $200,000 owed across many credit cards. He even sold his car that he owned outright and leased another vehicle on more debt. He hid his dark secret from his wife and pretended all was under control. He owed the tax office in excess of $500,000 with no way of paying it.

Bill projected optimism to his firm and clients, but his nerves were shot. He knew he was close to the edge.

Then the pressure got worse: he learned that based on his share of partnership profits, his tax bill was about to double. He had been paying down some debts from drawings but he was not even covering interest charges. He would lie awake at night, staring at the ceiling; or wake up at four in the morning with his mind racing, unable to shut it off; wondering, 'When is this thing going to turn around?'

After two years of constant anxiety, Bill finally began making money. He had some unexpected windfalls, found a little extra super he could cash in and did a deal with the ATO. This was a happy result. But often it is not. The reverse could have easily happened, especially if the Covid-19 pandemic or a global financial crisis had occurred at this time in his financial life.

We read every day in the press about the success of entrepreneurs. We dream about the Mark Zuckerbergs, the Bill Gateses and Elon Musks. But many of those entrepreneurs, like our Bill, harboured secret demons before they made it big. They struggled through moments of near-debilitating anxiety and despair – times when it seemed everything might crumble. Richard Branson talks about this in his book *Losing My Virginity* – how the dark clouds descended on him in his period of despair when he was fighting British Airways. They would later be fined £600,000 for their illegal actions against Virgin Airlines. It was little solace when his legal bills were continuing to mount with no way to fund them except by selling Virgin Records.

With the advent of the Beyond Blue and RUOK programs, there is currently a lot of help out there. But this has not always been the case. Admitting such sentiments, particularly for men, has traditionally been seen as a weakness. Many follow a strategy that is often preached by self-help gurus known as 'fake it 'til you make it'. What people see from the outside is a vibrant, successful entrepreneur. What the owner sees is pain and more pain. But they hide it.

I have known clients and colleagues who were unable to speak about their struggles or get the help they needed, or who shared nothing of their mental health and seemed perfectly okay. A colleague I worked with, in the weeks preceding their suicide, catalogued all their clients' login passwords and systems. They sent an email to a business associate to take over their clients and left the office for the day. A client of mine, faced with the pressure of mounting debts, took his own life. Both were tragic losses and rocked those that knew them. Both are very real examples of the enormous pressure and emotional cost faced by those running their own businesses.

Lately, more entrepreneurs have begun speaking out about their internal struggles in an attempt to combat the stigma around depression and anxiety that makes it hard for sufferers to seek help. In a deeply personal post called 'When Death Feels Like a Good Option,' Ben Huh, the CEO of the Cheezburger Network humour websites, wrote about his suicidal thoughts following a failed start-up in 2001.

Brad Feld, a managing director of the Foundry Group, started blogging in October about his latest episode of depression. The problem wasn't new – the prominent venture capitalist had struggled with mood disorders throughout his adult life – and he didn't expect much of a response. But then came the emails. Hundreds of them. Many were from entrepreneurs who had also wrestled with anxiety and despair. (For more of Feld's thoughts on depression, see his column, 'Surviving the Dark Nights of the Soul,' in *Inc.'s*.)

If you run a business, that probably all sounds familiar. It's a stressful job that can create emotional turbulence. In business there is a high risk of failure. In Australia, it is reported that some 80 per cent of all businesses fail in the first five years.

Entrepreneurs often juggle many roles and face countless setbacks – lost customers, disputes with partners, increased competition, staffing problems – all while struggling to make next week's payroll. Then there are the insolvency rules that can make the directors personally liable for tax debts and superannuation if they are paid late. Entrepreneurs face traumatic events every day: calls from disgruntled employees about their super not being paid, calls from the ATO requesting a payment plan be entered into, one that they know cannot be honoured.

Complicating matters, many business owners often make themselves less resilient by neglecting their health. They eat too much or too little. They don't get enough sleep. They fail to exercise. I recall meeting with one such entrepreneur in Sydney at a lunch. I commented how well he looked and if he had lost weight since we last met. He replied the years of board meetings and living out of hotel rooms had had an effect on his health. Now he was past that, he was not able to get his health back. What he didn't say was that the past years had taken a toll on him. He was part of one of the largest New Zealand corporate collapses in history. At the time he would have made the Guinness Book of Records for losing more money for his shareholders (and himself) than any other corporate liquidation. He had been hounded by the press for five years, was declared bankrupt and lost a large fortune. But now he was past it all. Things were going well and he had even remarried. So there can be light at the end of the tunnel. But in times of despair that can be hard to see.

To be an entrepreneur requires a single-minded determination, obsessive behaviour and a creative side to see the left-field solutions others do not. Because of this creative side, entrepreneurs often have mood swings. One day they are up, the next they are down. The days they are up they have massive energy. They can conquer the world and work non-stop for days on end. But when they are down, their demons come to the fore. What seeps in may include depression, despair, hopelessness, worthlessness, loss of motivation and suicidal thinking.

Some call it the downside of being up. The same passionate dispositions that drive founders heedlessly towards success can sometimes consume them. Business owners are 'vulnerable to the dark side of obsession,' suggest researchers from the Swinburne University of Technology in Melbourne, Australia. They conducted interviews with founders for a study about entrepreneurial passion. The researchers found that many subjects displayed signs of clinical obsession, including strong feelings of distress and anxiety, which have 'the potential to lead to impaired functioning,' they wrote in a paper published in the *Entrepreneurship Research Journal*.

Reinforcing that message is John Gartner, a practising psychologist who teaches at Johns Hopkins University Medical School. In his book *The Hypomanic Edge: The Link Between (a Little) Craziness and (a Lot of) Success in America*, Gartner argues that an often-overlooked temperament – hypomania – may be responsible for some entrepreneurs' strengths as well as their flaws. On the one hand it is what makes them great. On the other, when outside factors work against their aims and ambitions, it is what brings them down.

A milder version of mania, hypomania often occurs in the relatives of manic-depressives and affects an estimated 5 to

10 per cent of Americans. 'If you're manic, you think you are Jesus,' says Gartner. 'If you're hypomanic, you think you're God's gift to technology investing. We're talking about different levels of grandiosity but the same symptoms.'

Gartner theorises that there are so many hypomanic – and so many entrepreneurs – in the United States because the country's national character rose on waves of immigration. 'We're a self-selected population,' he says. 'Immigrants have unusual ambition, energy, drive and risk tolerance, which lets them take a chance on moving for a better opportunity. To travel many thousands of kilometres to a new country, often with no financial support, takes a certain level of risk taking and confidence in your abilities. If you seed an entire continent with them, you're going to get a nation of entrepreneurs.'

Though driven and innovative, those who are hypomanic are at much higher risk for depression than the general population, notes Gartner. Failure can spark these depressive episodes, of course, but so can anything that slows a hypomanic person's momentum. Think of them as being like border collies, a breed that constantly needs to run and round up sheep. Put a collie in a small suburban block and they will attack your furniture through boredom.

No matter what your psychological makeup, big setbacks in your business can knock you flat. Even experienced entrepreneurs have had the rug pulled out from under them.

Entrepreneurs struggle silently. There's a sense that they can't talk about it – that it's a weakness.

They often feel that their work defines them. That if they fail they will have nothing in their life. But the truth is, this is often not the case. They still have a life outside of their work.

Running a business will always be a wild ride, full of ups and downs. There are things entrepreneurs can do to help keep their lives from spiralling out of control. Most important, make time for your loved ones. Don't let your business squeeze out your connections with other people. When it comes to fighting off depression, relationships with friends and family can be powerful weapons. So don't be afraid to ask for help. See a mental health professional if you are experiencing symptoms of significant anxiety, post-traumatic stress disorder or depression.

When it comes to assessing risk, business owners have blind spots often big enough to drive a Mack truck through. They wear rose-coloured glasses, failing to see what is in front of them. The consequences can rock not only your bank account but also your stress levels. So set a limit for how much of your own money you're prepared to invest. Remember the 'pay yourself first' motto. Don't allow friends and family to lend you more than they can afford to lose.

On the personal side, ensure you get plenty of exercise, a healthy diet and adequate sleep. It also helps to cultivate an identity apart from your company. You need to expand your belief systems so you know that self-worth is not the same as net worth. Build balance in your life. Don't allow yourself to be so fixated on your business that there is no room for anything else. Whether you're raising a family, on the board of a local Lions Club, building model cars or going dancing on weekends, it's important to feel successful in areas unrelated to work.

So rethink what loss and what failure means. Look at the information from a different perspective. Instead of telling yourself 'I failed, the business failed, I'm a loser,' say 'Nothing ventured, nothing gained. Life is a constant process of trial and error. Don't exaggerate the experience.' As used to be said before the digital age, 'Today's news is tomorrow's fish and chip paper.'

Lastly, be open about your feelings – don't mask your emotions, even at the office. When you are willing to be emotionally honest, you can connect more deeply with the people around you. When you deny yourself and you deny what you're about, people can see through that. Being willing to be vulnerable is a very powerful trait in a leader.

35

You Are Not Your Work – The Problem with Passion

When you surround an army, leave an outlet free. Do not press a desperate foe too hard.
Sun Tzu, *The Art of War*

Many people in society, in particular business owners, equate success with money. Passion and work go hand in hand. Hence, they monetise their passion. It becomes a goal to create wealth because wealth means success. They lose sight of everything else. Sadly, this is a false reality. A person is not their work. Both are completely different.

In the *Harvard Business Review* on 10 April 2018 an article titled 'What Makes Entrepreneurs Burn Out' highlighted the relationship between entrepreneurship, burnout and two types of passion.

The first type was identified as 'harmonious passion', which leads to high levels of concentration, attention and absorption.

Some entrepreneurs, while they might feel overwhelmed by their work, take constant breaks and try to add flexibility to their work. They try to balance their job with their hobbies and families. Hence they do not experience any guilt or conflict especially when they are away from their work and attending to family matters.

The second type are so obsessive about their work that they can never relax. Emotionally they simply cannot live without their work. Such entrepreneurs struggle to pay attention, due to the constant conflict associated with work, neglecting family, eating correctly and knowing they do not have the balance right. The internal struggle can eat at their subconscious behaviour and cause them to act irrationally and have constant mood swings.

It is no surprise that 'obsessively passionate' entrepreneurs are far more at risk of burnout than their 'harmonious passion' counterparts.

We all need outlets and hobbies beyond our careers to be healthy and balanced human beings. One study showed that having a creative hobby, such as playing the piano or pottery, resulted in a measurable decrease in stress levels after the activity was completed. Studies have also found spending time walking or with nature has helped people become happier, more attentive and mentally present.

When you identify with your business, you set yourself up for various crises. Failure will be inevitable, as in business there will always be things that can go wrong. An entrepreneur never gets it right every single time. What's more, rejection is not a barrier to success, but rather a necessary part of the journey.

Relying on any single facet of your life for the entirety of your personal fulfilment is unhealthy and unrealistic. Mark Woeppel found solace in playing music during his business' downturn, saying, 'I used to be like, "My work is me." Then you fail. And you find out that your kids still love you. Your wife still loves you. Your dog still loves you.'

Kevin Eschleman, an assistant professor of psychology at San Francisco State University, showed that people who are more engaged in creative activities often scored 15 to 30 per cent higher on performance rankings than people who were less engaged: 'We found that, in general, the more you engage in creative activities, the better you'll do at work.'

So, importantly, a business entrepreneur needs to 'Make time for self-care'.

It's a vicious cycle: you're working so much that you forget to eat right or go to bed on time, so you wake up late, which puts you behind, so you work late again, and wake up at an even greater deficit.

Soon, you're burned out and want to avoid working altogether. Creating self-care habits isn't just a good idea in general, it can also do a lot to reduce stress and its side effects.

For example, take time for your own mental health. Be selfish about your own wellbeing. Turn off your 5 am alarm and allow yourself to wake naturally. Stop checking your emails every minute. Take a day off to be with family, have some 'me time'. Go for a walk or go to the gym. You will be far more productive and have a better mental attitude that will help you build or operate your business.

You might find it hard to justify spending an hour at the gym, 20 minutes a day meditating or even getting to bed at a reasonable hour. That trepidation is itself a symptom of the problem. Which is why picking just one or two of the self-care habits below and making incremental changes is so crucial.

- Breathe deeply – sends a message to your brain to calm down and relax.
- Be kind to yourself – focus on the positive aspects of your life. Don't beat yourself up when things don't work out. Focus on what you can do now and avoid dwelling on decisions you could have made. It changes your mindset to a positive framework and blocks negative energy.
- Take a break – it will give your brain a chance to recover from being overworked and stressed.
- Eat healthy and drink water – this not only leads to an overall healthier lifestyle, it increases your productivity. It also decreases your chances of developing obesity, diabetes, certain cancers and high blood pressure.

Self-care is important because it helps you maintain a healthy lifestyle. It helps you to produce feelings of happiness and transmit those feelings to the people around you. Self-care isn't meant to be disruptive or inconvenient to your life. It's there to relieve the pressure to succeed, make being active easier which leads to finding those illusive answers.

36

Entrepreneurs and Mental Health

This important chapter is adapted from an article written by Dr Prudence Gourguechon MD, Principal of Invantage Advising. It was originally published on Forbes.com and is reproduced with her kind permission. Dr Gourguechon is a psychiatrist, psychoanalyst and consultant based in Chicago, USA. In her consulting practice, she helps entrepreneurs and other business leaders navigate the psychological aspects of business. She is frequently quoted in the media as an expert on the psychological aspects of individual and group behaviour, as well as social, cultural and political phenomena. She has appeared in the Wall Street Journal *and* New York Times, *among many other media outlets, and has been interviewed on MSNBC's* The Last Word with Lawrence O'Donnell. *She is the author of* Uncommon Perspectives on the Psychology of Investing *and* Uncommon Perspectives on the Psychology of Leadership.

If this chapter raises any issues for you or someone you love, help is at hand. You can contact Lifeline Crisis Support Line (13 11 14), Beyond Blue Support Service (1300 224 636) or the National Debt Helpline (1800 007 007).

When things go wrong for a business owner or entrepreneur, the solution on how to handle the resulting mental anguish is not readily apparent. They often cannot see an end to the pain associated with this failure.

The biggest predictor of suicide may not be depression or thoughts about killing yourself (what people in mental health call 'suicidal ideation') but this feeling of being trapped.

They have bills that never seem to reduce. Creditors ring and the business owner wants to reassure them, feels sorry for them, but cannot avoid the fact that they will not be paid. Family put pressure on them for school fees, rent, and so on to be paid, but they can't find the money to do so.

There has been a shift in understanding about suicide that might just save some lives if colleagues, friends, family, psychiatrists, therapists and entrepreneurs themselves pay attention to it. When an entrepreneur indicates they have a feeling of being trapped, it's time for aggressive action – by the entrepreneur themselves if they can manage it, or by those who care if the person can't. While mental health care might be essential, it's equally important for the business to take care of the structural business issues that are contributing to the feeling of entrapment.

Entrepreneurs and Suicide Risk

There is no reliable data that compare the risk or rate of suicide among entrepreneurs to other comparable high-achieving and driven workers. But common sense says that the high-stress life, enormous uncertainty, exhaustion and risk of humiliation that every entrepreneur endures makes a case for increased caution.

The deaths of Anthony Bourdain and Kate Spade, as well as young and brilliant tech entrepreneurs Ilya Zhitomirskiy and Aaron Swartz, and an increasing willingness of a few brave individuals, like Olympian swimmers Michael Phelps and Ian Thorpe, to reveal their struggles with depression and thoughts of suicide are bringing the issue into the open.

Consider these four points of convergence between the life of an entrepreneur and increased risk of suicide:

Impulsivity

Entrepreneurs have higher rates of attention deficit disorder and bipolar disorder. It's unfortunate that these different neurological styles are associated with the word 'disorder'. They are invaluable variations of the human psyche, which create great strengths but also predictable vulnerabilities and sometimes illness.

The person with an ADD brain is restless, inquisitive, sometimes visionary, often relentless – and definitely impulsive. The person with a bipolar brain is capable of creative leaps, phenomenal energy, contagious inspiration and, also, is definitely impulsive.

Suicide is very often an impulsive act; suicidal ideation can occur just fifteen minutes before the act.

Depression

The higher incidence of bipolar disorder in entrepreneurs creates an increased risk of severe but usually highly treatable depression.

The mental state of someone who intends to commit suicide is characterised by unbearable psychological pain and a sense of hopelessness and helplessness. These mental states are typical of severe depression, which is the downside risk of having a bipolar brain. The hopelessness and helplessness of this kind of depression are actually delusions: fixed, false beliefs. I've seen many clients with these unbearable feelings recover from depression and discover that they don't feel hopeless or helpless at all, despite the fact that they are in the exact same external situation they were in when they could see no way out.

Social isolation

Social isolation is a risk factor for suicide, and it's also something that entrepreneurs and CEOs frequently feel. It's even worse to feel isolated when you are surrounded by people. You can still feel alone, as though no one understands or can help. It is said that it is lonely at the top. This is very true for business owners. They have no one to turn to for help or to seek counsel from. They worry about being judged if things have not gone as planned. So, they remain in social isolation.

Humiliation, Rejection and Failure

Intense humiliation is one of those unbearable psychological states that can be a contributor to suicidal actions. The very nature of entrepreneurship vastly increases the rate and intensity of experiences of humiliation, rejection and failure. An inability to tolerate these events may relate to long-standing personal vulnerabilities.

Prevention Advice for Boards, Colleagues and Entrepreneurs

Getting an entrepreneur out of a trap involves making business decisions.

Don't just send a 'trapped' person to 'get professional help' or urge them to take a leave of absence. Of course, trapped entrepreneurs should get treatment for depression when necessary – urgently if it is severe. They must also control any substance use associated with stress and coping mechanisms. Take time for talk therapy to help them deal with personality traits such as excessive vulnerability to humiliation. They may need to restore healthy practices related to sleep, rest, breaks and eating.

Don't be afraid to ask hard questions of those that appear to be at risk in your business, especially your boss. Ask others in the business if they are worried about the person, if they have a suicide plan. Also check if they have access to a firearm. If the answer is yes, take immediate steps to remove their access. Easy access to a lethal weapon is a well-known risk factor for fatal suicide attempts. If you combine access with lethal weapons and impulsivity, the possibility of lethal consequences rises significantly.

But take decisive business actions, too. There is no trap that needs to be fatal. However, the person who feels they are in one often can't see a way out. Don't offload the problem to family, friends or mental health professionals. See what structural changes need to be made in the business and the entrepreneur's role in it, and make sure these are not just talked about but rapidly implemented.

Ensure that every high-level, overstressed leader has someone to talk to, like a trusted, sophisticated personal advisor who is allowed inside the business and is also entrusted to talk to the Board and colleagues about critical changes that need to be made.

37

Your Power Within – How to Harness That Power

While the previous sections deal with tax and money tips, there is more to creating wealth and being successful than the analytical side of life. It's more than simply 1+1=2. All self-help books deal with this. In the universe, a strange power exists, a power that mystics and clairvoyants talk about. For entrepreneurs, they have a sort of sixth sense, a strong gut feeling on what works and what to avoid. They use this power without realising it to pull things together that are in alignment with their aims and wishes. The challenge is to recognise this power and be able to harness it when you need it.

Entrepreneurs know they have this intuitive power and know they sometimes need a quiet space to unleash it. I have seen Kerry Packer do exactly this with both the current affairs programme '60 Minutes' and World Series Cricket.

As an accountant and an analytical, practical person, the entire thrust of this chapter may seem strange and completely out of character. But I have had personal experience with this. Without realising it, I made the phone ring and manifested a takeover of a finance company I created. Of course, I didn't know it at that time.

This would again happen in a very unusual way. It was such a profound and unmistakable collision of events that there is no doubt that a greater power was at work. I was born on 6 January. From an astrological point of view, people tell me that I am a number six. I have never really placed much store in this sort of thing. But let me list the following events that actually occurred, and you can be the judge.

We moved from NSW to Queensland in late 2013. Add this number and the answer is six. Initially, we rented a house until we worked out where we wanted to live. When it came time to purchase a house, we started to look around. I remember lying in bed and doing some internet searches on properties for sale. I was looking for a property that had subdivision potential, was on a large block of land or a corner or that was big enough to allow a duplex to be built. Something that we could make money on, as well as provide us a place to live while we did the development. I had this thought in my head when I started to look at properties for sale. A house in Bowen Hills caught my attention. Being so close to the city, close to my office and in a good area, I thought it would be above my budget. I wrote down the address and thought I would drive by on the way to visit another house at Hamilton. I went by the house at about 12.25 on a Saturday morning, not really thinking about the time. I couldn't believe my luck – it was open for inspection from 12.00 to 12.30. My wife was in the car, and after much persuading, we both did a quick one-minute inspection. We didn't even look downstairs. I thought the house had potential, but it was very neglected and needed a lot of work. It was over 100 years old and tired.

After a follow-up call from the agent, I decided to make an offer that was within my budget. The offer was a little low and not accepted, but as the house was up for auction, I decided to attend the auction and bid. I was successful and obtained the house at a very reasonable price given the size of the block of land. The house was on three titles, and it seemed possible to subdivide one block off. It was also heritage listed, so it was obvious there would be some hurdles. The scary part is that the settlement date, as per the contract, was 60 days after the auction. This fell exactly on 6 January, and we did actually settle on that day. To further compound this, the house number was 15, which adds up to the number 6. I didn't even notice this at the time. It has proved to be the best decision we have ever made and has nearly doubled in value in four years.

This was the second property we purchased in Queensland. The first property was to be our office. The number of this building was 33, which again adds up to 6. Both of these purchases have turned out to be extremely profitable investments.

The reason I wanted to relate this simple story was to prove that there is a greater power out there. There is a power that you can manifest to bring into your life the things you need to either solve your problems, find success or achieve the life you want.

So how do you use it? How do you find that power within?

When you are focused on what you want, the universe somehow seems to bring those things into your peripheral vision. As an example, when you are thinking of buying a new BMW, every second car you see seems to be a BMW. You are more focused and aware of the thing you want. When you are single-minded and determined, opportunities just seem to come to you. Yes, you need to act, but be aware that they will come to you. In my experience, I have seen many wealthy people seize new ventures, not be afraid to take a measured risk and act quickly on opportunities.

When something comes past your peripheral vision that is aligned with your goals, plans and ambitions, jump at it. Don't hesitate. If you do, it will be a case of 'I wish I had done such and such.'

38

Millionaire Mindset – The Holdbacks

We spend over 61 per cent of our awake time in our business. If your business is not successful, then your life will be less than optimal. While many factors contribute to running a successful business, as highlighted in the earlier chapters, one thing stands out. That is the mindset of the entrepreneur business owner. Is the business owner himself or herself the problem?

In my career I have dealt with many thousands of business owners. When I consider the successful business owners I have worked with, I would categorise them into two broad categories:

- The first make money constantly, lose it and then make it again. They seesaw between success and failure but always seem to come back. They believe they will always be wealthy and live a wealthy lifestyle.
- The second are those who continually fail and can't pick themselves up. Their life is like a train wreck, going from failure to failure. They have many companies that go into liquidation, usually owing the taxation department money, superannuation for staff is not paid and the list goes on. In the process, they take all of their family and friends down with them.

You might say the above two are the same, and that luck may have a part to play. But they are not the same. The first category knows that they can always create again if things go against them. The second category go from failure to failure and never seem to have the success the first category does.

Unfortunately, I cannot name the clients who fall into the above categories for confidentiality reasons, but I always feel sad and have tried to help them. I've been an avid reader of self-help books from an early age, and while I do not think I know it all, I can recognise the symptoms. In most cases, it comes down to mindset and self-beliefs. I have always been a believer that we make our own luck. In the words of Anthony Robbins, what the mind 'can conceive, the mind can achieve'. Henry Ford said, 'Whether you believe it is right or believe it is wrong, you will be correct.'

I want to take a section out of Mark Anastasi's book titled *Unleash the Millionaire Within*, as he expresses this better than I can. In Chapter 3 on how to 'Identify and Eliminate Roadblocks', he lists many of the things that can hold a person back from being successful. They are self-sabotaging beliefs. When success comes, people often push it away, as subconsciously, these beliefs will kick in. Until you identify these sabotaging beliefs, you will not be able to change your situation to achieve the true success that awaits you. Kerry Packer had no holdbacks. Early in life, his father treated him badly, put him down and ridiculed him. But he pulled himself up and changed his mindset. I know you are thinking that's okay for someone like Kerry. But the truth is, many people who came from poverty did exactly that. Anthony Robbins is a good example.

When I talk to clients (which I do every day) about their business and their beliefs, I see many items on the list that Mark Anastasi quotes. 'Many people stumble along blind their entire lives, wondering why their lives simply don't work. Health problems, money problems, relationship problems, weight problems. These are just a few of what the average person goes through,' Mark explains.

People go through life sabotaging themselves with conflicting inner desires. They might consciously believe they 'want more money' but they actually believe deep down that their friends won't like them anymore if they make more money than them.

On page 108 of his book, Mark listed out 33 limiting beliefs about money, which to a business owner equates to success. These are listed below:

- You have to be born wealthy to be a millionaire.
- I am not educated enough.
- It takes luck to be a millionaire.
- You have to be a crook to get rich.
- I'm too old to start.
- It's hard to make money … money doesn't grow on trees.
- To make money, you have to take advantage of other people.
- To get rich, you have to take it from someone else, and they'll have less. It's not fair.
- I can't afford to start my own business.
- What if I fail? What will people think of me? I'll be ridiculed.
- What if I make a lot of money and lose it all? Then I'm really a failure.
- I'm afraid … what if I fail? (… then I'm really not good enough).
- I'm afraid of rejection. What if people say no? What if people don't like my product?
- If I make more money than my friends, they won't like me anymore.
- It's not fair that some people make more money than others … so I'll remain poor.
- I'm not good enough. I don't deserve more money and happiness.

- All the good ideas are taken.
- People fight over money, so it is better to not have any.
- Money is the root of all evil, so it is better if I don't have any.
- In order to make more money, I'll have to work harder. If I won't have time to enjoy it, why even try?
- To make money, you need to be really smart, and I'm not smart enough.
- Money can't buy you happiness; money can't buy you love.
- If I make a lot of money, I'll get sucked in. What about my spiritual side?
- If I get rich, everyone is going to want a handout.
- Others need it more than me. I don't deserve it.
- I'm afraid about money because … I've had it in the past and lost it. I don't want to experience that again.
- I feel guilty about having a better life than my mother.
- Having too much is a bad thing; you'll be spoilt rotten.
- Look at those uneducated people who suddenly made a lot of money in Poland. They still have hay sticking out of their shoes … They're probably drug dealers.
- I am comfortable and satisfied with having just enough to get by … like my mum.
- Money goes to people who are materialistic and lack human qualities, screwing people along the way.
- Making $1 million a year is impossible! It scares me.
- I'm afraid of money. It goes as quick as it comes.

Anyone reading the above will be able to offer exceptions to these statements. But they are often subconscious beliefs that you are not aware are holding you back.

The purpose of this chapter is to bring them to your attention. Maybe just one reader will resonate with the above and know what needs to be addressed to stop these roadblocks to success. In his book, Mark quoted Brian Tracy stating, 'Change your thinking and you will change your life.' If you suffer from any of the above limiting beliefs, there are many ways to get help in order to resolve this problem. The first is, of course, to recognise that these limited, self-sabotaging beliefs are holding you back. Identify them and then embark on a massive reading and studying exercise. Read as many self-help books as you can. Books like Stephen Covey's *7 Habits of Highly Successful People*, Dale Carnegie's *How to Win Friends and Influence People* and many more of the great books of our time. You can even attend seminars that resonate with the above self-help genres.

Go out of your way to get to know successful people and talk to them. They are always willing to share their secrets. More importantly, be proactive in educating yourself. After all, you are the greatest person you know.

You have in your hands the ability to do anything you want and achieve anything you want. You just need to do it.

Conclusion

The Western world has a strong system of taxation that takes away your choice and gives this to a central government who decide how they will spend your money. But entrepreneurs do not see it that way. To them, taxation is a game, like being in business, that they want to win at. A game of using the system to minimise their contribution to the taxation system and then be able to build wealth and assist those less fortunate in the way they choose.

These two sides – making money and keeping it – deal with running a successful business and then retaining as much of those profits as possible, without the burden of taxation.

There are pitfalls and personal costs of entrepreneurship, something a budding entrepreneur needs to be mindful of if they are to embark upon this journey. It is a fact that just being in business means there is a strong chance that things will not go as planned. Remember, some 85 per cent of businesses fail in the first five years. The lot of a business owner is a hard one. Dealing with failure has consequences that can lead to depression and the feeling of being trapped. Not knowing who to turn to can put enormous strain on an owner's mental health, leading to drastic decisions and, tragically, in some cases even suicide. However, if you get it right more than 50 per cent of the time, you are doing well.

We all have dreams and ambitions. It is not a person's dreams that fail them, it is the tools required to put those dreams into action. It is here that many fall short. By using the knowledge in this book, I hope you can learn what it takes to run a successful business, how to avoid the traps and pitfalls, and how to use the tax system to retain as much of those profits as possible.

Acknowledgements

First, I want to thank Pat Mesiti for pushing me to write the first edition of this book. While we all hate paying tax, Pat felt that I had a message that needed to be told and that my experience – including working for Kerry Packer, at that time Australia's richest man – was so unique I had an obligation to share it with others. Pat also felt that the manner in which I have helped many small business owners reduce their tax by simply being alert to their issues was worth telling.

I also wish to thank my wife, Marsha, for putting up with me for over 40 years. Yes, there have been some highs and some lows, not to mention the long hours at the office.

Corinna Essa, thank you for assisting me with the first edition of this book to get the content right and the marketing plans.

Mark Anastasi, thank you for your enlightening book and ideas on the millionaire mindset, and for allowing me to reproduce some of those ideas in Part 5.

In researching the material for this book, I have reviewed the websites of the Australian Taxation Office, Chartered Accountants Australia & New Zealand, and CPA Australia. Some of the content of this book is a result of that research and some of the material being of a public nature, has been reproduced in this book. Where that has been done, every effort has been made to attribute the information to its source.

Lastly, I want to thank my many business clients, who have been far more than clients. In many cases, they have become lifelong friends. I have loved working with you and loved being challenged to find solutions.